DISCOVER YOUR CALLING

A 30-Day Blueprint to Finding Purpose

By:

Maya Lynne robinson

Copyright October 2024 by Maya Lynne Robinson

All rights reserved. Printed in The United States of America No part of this book may be used or reproduced without written permission except in the case of brief quotations included in articles and reviews.

For information contact us at:

liveintruthinfo@gmail.com

ISBN: 978-1-7374700-6-9

DISCOVER YOUR CALLING

A 30-Day Blueprint to Finding Purpose

Cover and author photo by Allen Zaki

1st Edition

TABLE OF CONTENTS

INTRODUCTION 4

SELF-CARE 20

INTUITION 86

PURPOSE 160

DIVERSIFY YOUR BUSINESS 194

EVALUATION 232

MODULE 1
INTRODUCTION

M.I.S.S. METHOD

I am in my third transformation in this life. I always knew I was born to diverse how I show upon my purpose, and it would manifest four times, the third being the most impactful. And here I am, now in the third one. The first was when I found my passion for the performing arts. The second was when I found my passion as a healer, and now, as I move into my teacher/creator phase, I realize that I have unknowingly been leading myself to this phase for as long as I can remember. I have always been inquisitive and I don't follow the crowd, I follow my gut. Sometimes my gut leads me down a dark or lonely path, but I always realize it's to shake me out of my comfort zone and help me elevate in life. We elevate three ways- by helping others, helping ourselves and helping the world. To get to the levels of execution or manifestation, we must know who we are, trust ourselves, figure out our purpose, and execute a plan.

It takes courage to stand in the light and be scrutinized, judged, admired, and revered while living in this world nowadays. You see, the thing we shy away from the most, the truth of who we are, is often the one thing we need to embrace. This deals specifically with the NORTH Node. My North node requires me to stay in the spotlight... a place I was never too comfortable in.

What does this have to do with the MISS Method? Everything. I grew up being told I was too loud, too much, too opinionated and that that behavior would not be tolerate or embraced. Free thinking and inclusivity were not synonymous in my upbringing, and so I slowly became who others wanted - a tame version of myself. Someone who focused on taking care of others before myself and pushing down my feelings and boundaries as to not be alienated by everyone who came into my life. My spirit was dying and crying. But I conformed and tamed myself so much that you might miss me if you weren't looking hard enough. I could blend into a room, and that was my conditioning. I was deep in my SOUTH NODE, collaboration. I desperately wanted to belong somewhere with someone, any one.

M.I.S.S. METHOD - PT 2

My purpose meant I would have to stand in the light alone and trust myself each and every time. I had to learn to not dim my light, figure out what I liked and wanted in life and heal childhood trauma. Who else can relate?

The final straw for me was 2023. A lot of things and people became illuminated to me as not being for my best interest, even if I was for theirs. The M.I.S.S. Method taught me a lot about the difference between intuition and discernment. Though I might be in the best interest of other people, they may not be in my best interest. Learning how to judge well who I should pour into and who I shouldn't has been a painfully long and arduous lesson. I needed to fill my cup up because I did not receive equal reciprocity from what I poured into others. It was time for me to Make Internal Spiritual Shifts (M.I.S.S.)

This method has been eight years in the making, and now it's time to share it. I'm looking forward to sharing what this last experiment taught me as a participant and a visionary. I hope our experiences (those brave souls over the last eight years) help you step into your greatest power and person.

M.I.S.S. METHOD - PT 3

The M.I.S.S. method has four modules and two areas for self-evaluation. The first section self-evaluates the raw, vulnerable, and honest YOU. It prepares you to open up and embrace the journey.

Module 1: Making- What is my value?

Module 2: Internal - What do I feel?

Module 3: Spiritual - What is my purpose?

Module 4: Shifts - What is my plan?

The final section is the re-evaluation of self after the process and noticing and celebrating your path.

If you can't spend an hour a day for the next 30 days setting your life up for success, you are wasting your time, resources, and happiness. Get out of your way! Take care of yourself.

"When I learn who I am and my boundaries and needs, I have the tools to teach people how to treat me. I create a deeper understanding of my purpose."

Get ready for the rebirth.

Sending Light and Love,

Maya Lynne Robinson

TRINITY-THE RULES

Analyzing myself can be uncomfortable.

Listed below are the three traits I must adhere to in order for this course to work for me. I will stay open to honest self-evaluation.

Consistency | Discipline | Safety

I take it day-by-day, and show up for myself. I celebrate the milestones along the way to the big goal.

I finish what I start. I do not give myself permission to walk away from the work.

I am doing the work on my own and at my own pace. I share with whom I want when I am ready.

SELF CARE

I will invest one hour a day in my care. When I learn what need, I am able to teach others my needs. Self-care is not selfishness. I can't take care of myself when I always put the needs of others before my own. To best take care of others, I must first take care of myself.

Investing at least one hour into self-care each day is of paramount importance. It is a powerful tool for preserving my physical, mental, and emotional well-being, preventing burnout, and reducing stress. Self-care contributes to better physical health, improved relationships, and a healthier work-life balance. By recognizing and honoring my needs, I lay the foundation for a more fulfilling, balanced, and joyful life.

This is the bare minimum and the first step to self- actualization.

ABOUT THE PROCESS

I have learned that when I invest in my foundation, the inner workings of myself, I yield the highest rewards, which money cannot buy - happiness, integrity, freedom and peace.

Here are a few benefits of doing this process in 30 days.

Enhanced Decision-Making:

Sharpen my ability to make better decisions. Improved intuition can lead to more confident and effective choices in various aspects of life, such as career, relationships, and personal development.

Stress Reduction:

Learn to trust and develop my intuition to reduce stress and navigate challenges with greater ease and resilience.

Personal Growth and Self-Discovery:

Create a pathway to personal growth and self-discovery. I may be seeking to understand myself better, uncover hidden talents, and explore my potential through the development of intuitive abilities.

Professional and Creative Enhancement:

Boost my performance in the workplace or my creative endeavors. Strengthening intuition can lead to increased innovation, problem-solving skills, and a deeper understanding of clients, colleagues, or audiences.

ENJOY THE JOURNEY

I am allowed to grow, which includes changing my mind about who I am and what I want in life. The answer, my purpose, will never be wrong if it brings me fulfillment.

This course focuses on exploring who I am NOW and what I CURRENTLY would like to pursue. It is in-depth regarding present thinking, future planning, and past healing.

What are you looking forward to the most about this journey and why?

- » **Past Healing**
- » **Present Thinking**
- » **Future Planning**

SELF DISCOVERY

I will feel pretty great at times and pretty bad others. What shows up when I do the work is my higher self and shadow self. This means coming to terms with triggers due to generational traumas, curses and core value differences, as well as realizing what I have overcome and healed through. I will be gentle with myself. I will show myself grace as I learn to intuit these new thoughts and feelings.

There's is a lot to discover about myself. I will keep all of this information in one spot to reference later. I will take my time, dig deep, and be honest with myself. I will use the worksheets for reference. That's the way this process works.

I will return to this page whenever I am feeling a bit stagnant during the process.

Do I have additional thoughts?

HOW DO I FEEL?

I have learned to shelve my own feelings in favor of everyone else's. But I come first. My feelings matter.

This page is a safe and non-judgmental space: I feel comfortable expressing myself without fear of criticism or judgment. My feelings are valid.

I HONOR MY NEEDS

I will invest one hour a day in my care. When I learn what I need, I am able to teach others my needs. Self-care is not selfishness. I can't take care of myself when I always put the needs of others before my own. I must first take care of myself to best take care of others.

Investing at least one hour into self-care each day is of paramount importance. It is a powerful tool for preserving my physical, mental, and emotional well-being, preventing burnout, and reducing stress. Self-care improves physical health, relationships, and a healthier work-life balance. I lay the foundation for a more fulfilling, balanced, and joyful life by recognizing and honoring my needs.

This is the bare minimum and the first step to self-actualization.

WHAT ARE MY HOPES FOR THIS PROCESS?

I am ready to begin releasing what no longer serves my life, figure out who I am, and what I want to do with the rest of my time here.

I believe in miracles. If I can think it, I can achieve it. Write, in-depth, what I want from this process.

MEETING MYSELF

I am made of light and dark qualities. My free will, in both forms, creates my personality, therefore creating my reality. How would I feel if I took a moment to be still and in my own company for a bit? Do I like who I am? Do I recognize myself, or is a stranger staring at me in the mirror?

WHAT ENERGIZES ME?

To figure this out, I am required to move before I am ready. The anticipation of charting a course for my life, figuring out why certain things work and others don't, and reflecting on the growth during the process are some of the things I have to look forward to creating. I will take this step-by-step.

What are my light and dark qualities that I wish to address?

WHO AM I?

I am learning who I am and teaching others how to value me.

Most people do not know who they are outside of people or professions in their lives. Who am I, outside of what I do and who I commit my personal time and energy towards?

MODULE 2
SELF-CARE

SELF-CARE ASSESSMENT

Practicing self-care is a crucial aspect of overall well-being, and understanding the factors that have brought me to this point is essential for successful implementation. Several internal and external factors contribute to the recognition and prioritization of self-care. Internally, it begins with self-awareness, where I recognize my physical, mental, and emotional needs.

This self-awareness may stem from personal experiences such as burnout, stress, or a desire for personal growth and fulfillment. External factors can include societal influences, such as an increased focus on mental health and self-care in mainstream media, conversations, and social platforms. Supportive relationships, whether with family, friends, or professionals, can also play a significant role in fostering the importance of self-care. Life events, such as major transitions, losses, or health challenges, can serve as wake-up calls that highlight the need for self-care.

Societal and cultural shifts towards valuing holistic well-being have encouraged me to embrace self-care as a means of self-preservation and personal growth. By acknowledging and understanding these internal and external factors, I can better understand my motivations and lay a solid foundation for successfully integrating self-care practices into my life.

SELF-CARE CHECK IN

Here's a self-care assessment addressing each chakra:

1. Root Chakra (Muladhara):

Am I able to meet my basic needs with ease?

2. Sacral Chakra (Swadhisthana):

How connected do I feel to my emotions and sensuality?

3. Solar Plexus Chakra (Manipura):

Do I feel empowered to pursue my goals and dreams?

4. Heart Chakra (Anahata):

How open do I feel to giving and receiving love?

5. Throat Chakra (Vishuddha):

Do I feel heard and understood by others?

6. Third Eye Chakra (Ajna):

Do I feel a sense of purpose and direction in my life?

7. Crown Chakra (Sahasrara):

How connected do I feel to my spirituality or higher consciousness?

If any of these were not easy to answer, I will take this week to focus extra on those chakras/areas of my life that require growth to reach my highest potential.

SELF-CARE CHECK IN

Reflect on my current time management practices, analyze how I allocate my time, and identify areas for improvement and strategies to enhance my time management skills. Use extra spaces for additional practices.

CURRENT

Time	
	HEALTH AND WELL-BEING
	FAMILY/FRIENDS
	HOBBIES
	REST

Time	
	WORK
	SERVICE/SUPPORT
	FINANCIAL PLANNING

PROJECTED

Time	
	HEALTH AND WELL-BEING
	FAMILY/FRIENDS
	HOBBIES
	REST

Time	
	WORK
	SERVICE/SUPPORT
	FINANCIAL PLANNING

IDENTIFYING SELF

I am made up of core values, morals, and belief systems.

Addressing my values is an opportunity to sit and think about what ideas and actions are most important, still important, or have yet to be addressed. I will identify all six intentions and hold myself accountable for working on the top three for maximum self-care results.

Examples of daily self-care practices:

Physical - exercise 30 min

Emotional - journal for 10 min

Spiritual - meditate for 2 min

Intellectual - learn a new word

Social - call a friend

Environmental* - share a funny video

* Environmental self-care is any action you take to improve the world's conditions.

Reminder: Each day represents a different chakra to focus on. I will keep this in mind while doing the work.

SELF-CARE/ INTENTION

"Take big steps through big doors with big intentions."

Write down all the different ways I can show myself care.

PHYSICAL	EMOTIONAL	SPIRITUAL

INTELLECTUAL	SOCIAL	ENVIRONMENTAL

NOTES

SELF-CARE/ INTENTION

"Take big steps through big doors with big intentions."

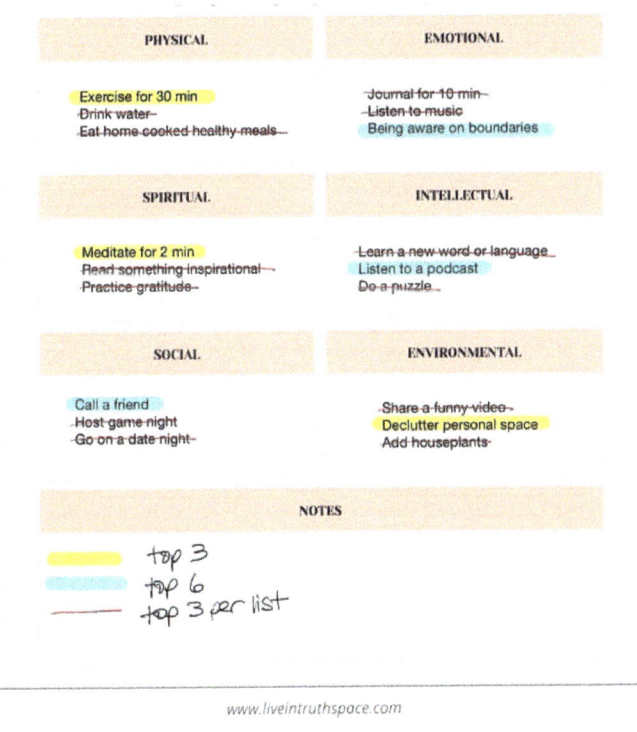

PHYSICAL
- Exercise for 30 min
- Drink water
- Eat home cooked healthy meals

EMOTIONAL
- Journal for 10 min
- Listen to music
- Being aware on boundaries

SPIRITUAL
- Meditate for 2 min
- Read something inspirational
- Practice gratitude

INTELLECTUAL
- Learn a new word or language
- Listen to a podcast
- Do a puzzle

SOCIAL
- Call a friend
- Host game night
- Go on a date night

ENVIRONMENTAL
- Share a funny video
- Declutter personal space
- Add houseplants

NOTES

— top 3
— top 6
— top 3 per list

www.liveintruthspace.com

DAY ONE
SALT BATH

On Day One, we start with work on your crown chakra. The salt bath is used as a purifier/detox element for clearer consciousness and spirit. Salt baths help balance the crown chakra by promoting relaxation and cleansing on an energetic level.

The high mineral content in salt, such as magnesium, potassium, and calcium, offers many advantages for our bodies. Salt baths promote muscle relaxation, reduce inflammation, and alleviate stress. The minerals in the salt are easily absorbed through the skin, providing a natural way to replenish and balance electrolytes. Salt baths can help detoxify the body by drawing out toxins and impurities through osmosis. They nourish the body, creating a soothing effect on the mind, promoting mental clarity and tranquility.

Incorporating regular salt baths into self-care routines is a simple yet powerful way to support overall well-being. Before incorporating salt baths into your routine, consult with a healthcare professional if you have any specific health concerns or conditions.

RECOMMENDATION

TAKE A SALT BATH 2-4X A MONTH FOR 20-30 MINUTES

SALT BATHS AS SPIRITUAL PROTECTION

You want to start by protecting your spirit and body. This is how we support the crown chakra. Salt baths are often associated with spiritual protection because salt is believed to have purifying and cleansing properties in many cultures and spiritual practices. Taking a salt bath is thought to help cleanse negative energy from the body and aura, creating a sense of spiritual protection. Additionally, the act of immersing oneself in warm water can promote relaxation and inner peace, which can also contribute to a sense of spiritual well-being and protection.

Here's a simple spiritual salt bath ritual you can try:

1. Gather your materials: You'll need Epsom salt or sea salt (preferably non-iodized), essential oils (optional), candles, and any crystals or herbs you'd like to incorporate.

2. Set the mood: Light your candles and dim the lights to create a calming atmosphere. Play soft music or nature sounds if desired.

3. Prepare your bath: Fill your bathtub with warm water. Add a handful of salt to the water, stirring it gently to dissolve.

4. Optional additions: If you like, you can add a few drops of essential oils like lavender, rosemary, or sage for added relaxation and purification. You can also place crystals or herbs around the edge of the tub or float them in the water.

5. Set your intention: As you soak in the bath, take a few moments to set your intention for the ritual. Visualize yourself being cleansed of any negative energy and surrounded by a protective aura.

6. Relax and soak: Step into the bath and allow yourself to relax fully. Close your eyes and focus on your breath, letting go of any tension or stress.

7. Visualize: Visualize the salt water enveloping you in a protective barrier, cleansing away any negativity or unwanted energies.

8. Stay as long as you like: Spend as much time in the bath as you need to feel fully cleansed and rejuvenated. When you're ready, slowly rise from the water and towel off gently.

9. Ground yourself: After the bath, take a moment to ground yourself by standing barefoot on the earth or holding onto a grounding crystal like black tourmaline.

10. Express gratitude: Before concluding the ritual, express gratitude for the cleansing and protection you've received. Blow out the candles and take a few moments to bask in the feeling of peace and renewal.

Remember, the most important aspect of any spiritual ritual is your intention and belief in its power. Adjust the ritual to suit your preferences and intuition, and feel free to incorporate any additional elements that resonate with you.

SALT BATH

FILL OUT AFTER YOUR SALT BATH

Today I am grateful for:

My Top 3 Goals

Schedule

To Do List

- [ ]
- [ ]
- [ ]
- [ ]
- [ ]
- [ ]
- [ ]
- [ ]
- [ ]

How was my salt bath?

SELF-CARE- DAY ONE

Today, I decided to take a bath. I've done this countless times, but today felt different. I left the glass of wine and the iPad behind, choosing instead to sit in stillness, alone with my thoughts. It was deeply uncomfortable—being fully present with myself in the quiet. But as the moments passed, something profound began to unfold. I realized that this quiet space is what God has intended for me all along. How can I hear the whispers meant for me if I'm always drowning them out with distractions? The bath became more than just a ritual; it felt like a calling to reconnect, to quiet the mind, body, and spirit, and to start healing from the inside out. As the salts and minerals worked to draw toxins from my body, my mind began to clear, releasing the day's clutter and making way for peace. My spirit, usually tucked away beneath all the noise, found a moment to breathe, to rest. When people say, "rest your weary mind," I think this is what they mean: a true reset.

Today, as I sank into the warmth, I realized that this time isn't just for me; it's also for the ones I love. If I'm not here—fully present and recharged—who will be there to support them? People might find substitutes in my absence, but the care I give myself is irreplaceable. I'm learning that this pause, this moment of stillness, is as vital as anything else.

So, I'll keep showing up for myself, even when it's uncomfortable. I'll keep making time to be still, to heal, and to trust that, in these quiet moments, I'm investing in something far greater than relaxation. I'm nurturing my soul.

THOUGHTS

THOUGHTS

DAY TWO
LIGHTEN UP

Day Two, we work with the sacral chakra. Introducing brighter colors and lively patterns into your wardrobe can resonate with the sacral chakra's essence. Color therapy, also known as chromotherapy, is based on the idea that different colors can have a profound effect on our emotions, mood, and overall well-being.

When it comes to healing the sacral chakra, which is associated with creativity, passion, and emotional expression, using specific colors can be therapeutic.

These vibrant choices can ignite feelings of passion, creativity, and emotional expression, aligning with the sacral chakra's association with sensuality and pleasure. By embracing bold clothing selections, you invite a sense of playfulness and spontaneity into your life, fostering a deeper connection to your emotions and creative instincts. Infusing your wardrobe with vibrant hues can harmonize with the sacral chakra's energy, bringing you a sense of joy, vitality, and emotional well-being.

So next time you're picking out an outfit, why not reach for something bright and cheerful? You'll not only look great, but you'll also be inviting a whole lot of positivity and fresh perspectives into your day!

RECOMMENDATION

PLAN YOUR WARDROBE FOR THE WEEK THAT INCORPORATES LIGHT AND BRIGHT COLORS.

LIGHTEN UP TO SEE A DIFFERENT PERSPECTIVE

Here's a step-by-step process for picking a bright, colorful, and beautiful wardrobe for the week.

1. Check the Weather Forecast: Start by checking the weather forecast for the week ahead. This will help you plan your outfits based on the expected temperatures and conditions.

2. Assess Your Schedule: Take a look at your schedule for the week and consider any events or activities you have planned. This will help you choose appropriate outfits for each day.

3. Choose Your Base Pieces: Select a few basic clothing items, like tops, bottoms, and dresses, in neutral colors such as white, black, or denim. These will serve as the foundation for your colorful outfits.

4. Pick Your Color Palette: Decide on a color palette for the week. Choose a mix of bright and cheerful colors that reflect your mood and personality. Think vibrant yellows, bold reds, playful pinks, and serene blues.

5. Mix and Match: Mix and match your base pieces with colorful clothing items from your wardrobe. Experiment with different combinations to create visually interesting outfits.

6. Accessorize: Add accessories such as statement jewelry, scarves, belts, or shoes in complementary colors to complete your looks. Accessories are a great way to add pops of color to your outfits and tie everything together.

7. Try Everything On: Once you've selected your outfits for

the week, try everything on to make sure you feel comfortable and confident in each ensemble.

8. Make Adjustments: Make any necessary adjustments to your outfits, such as swapping out pieces that don't work well together or adding layers for extra warmth if needed.

9. Finalize Your Wardrobe: Once you're happy with your outfits for the week, hang them up or lay them out in your closet so they're ready to go each morning.

By following these steps, you'll be able to create a bright, colorful, and beautiful wardrobe for the week that reflects your personal style and brightens your mood!

LIGHTEN UP

COMPLETE AFTER YOU SELECT YOUR OUTFITS FOR THE WEEK.

Schedule

My Top 3 Goals

Schedule

To Do List

- [ ]
- [ ]
- [ ]
- [ ]
- [ ]
- [ ]
- [ ]
- [ ]
- [ ]

What outfits did I pick? Why?

Discover Your Calling

LIGHTEN UP-DAY TWO

Every time I reach Day Two of this challenge, I feel a spark of happiness ignite. I spend so much time in black clothes—my comfort zone—that stepping out of it feels both refreshing and revealing. It makes me wonder: what other colors, what pieces, have I been avoiding? Why have I surrounded myself with so few light shades, and what does that say about my mood or mindset?

My closet is styled like a boutique, which lets me "shop" from home, picking out pieces I'd forgotten about. As I try on different outfits, I feel my mood shift with each new look. This time felt different, though. I was genuinely excited to see my clothes in a new light. It prompted me to reflect on what I've been holding onto, what I need to release, and why. Why don't I explore my wardrobe like this more often, outside of this 30-day challenge?

With three more bags of clothes and shoes loaded in my car, I felt a tangible sense of evolution in my style. I'm drawn to light, bright colors now. So, when I slipped back into my usual monochromatic black outfit—my staple that always feels safe and sophisticated—it didn't feel the same. Usually, black brings me confidence; it's sleek, classic, and easy. But today, something felt off. My energy felt heavy, like the clothes were dimming my light.

That's when it clicked—my spirit is lightening, and it's showing up in how I dress. Trying on those bright, airy pieces first made me realize just how much the dark shades were weighing me down. It's these small observations that signal real growth. By paying attention to how I feel, I can see how much I'm changing, evolving from the inside out.

DAY THREE
ROUTINES

On Day Three, we delve into the third eye chakra, where our morning and evening routines intertwine with profound significance. Starting the day with practices like meditation or journaling awakens intuition and clarity, fostering a deeper sense of awareness. Evening reflection nurtures self-awareness and insight,  instilling trust in our inner wisdom. Bedtime dreamwork taps into subconscious messages, reinforcing intuitive guidance. Mindfulness practices throughout the day sustain the activation of the third eye chakra, enhancing perception and spiritual insight. Together, these routines support a balanced and heightened awareness, enriching daily experiences with clarity and intuition.

This is the moment I embrace the journey ahead, where my commitment becomes unwavering. I will not allow myself to stop today. Embracing change is essential. If I already have a morning and evening routine, this is the time I will switch things up!

RECOMMENDATION

WRITE DOWN YOUR IDEAL MORNING AND EVENING ROUTINES AND START IMMEDIATELY.

CREATING SUCCESSFUL ROUTINES

Creating successful morning and evening routines can set the tone for your entire day and help you wind down at night. Here's a step-by-step process to help you establish routines that work for you:

Morning Routine:

1. Set Your Intentions: Start by setting intentions for your day. Take a moment to think about what you want to accomplish and how you want to feel.

2. Wake Up Refreshed: Aim to wake up at a consistent time each morning to regulate your body's internal clock. Start by setting your alarm for a time that allows you to get enough sleep.

3. Hydrate: Drink a glass of water as soon as you wake up to rehydrate your body after a night of sleep.

4. Movement and Exercise: Incorporate some form of movement or exercise into your morning routine to get your blood flowing and boost your energy levels.

5. Mindfulness Practice: Take a few moments for mindfulness or meditation to center yourself and set a positive tone for the day ahead.

6. Healthy Breakfast: Eat a nutritious breakfast to fuel your body and brain for the day ahead. Choose foods that are high in protein, fiber, and healthy fats to keep you feeling satisfied and energized. Plan Your Day: Take a few minutes to review your schedule and priorities for the day. Make a to-do list or set intentions for what you

want to accomplish.

Evening Routine:

1. Wind Down: Start winding down at least an hour before bedtime. Turn off electronic devices and engage in calming activities like reading, journaling, or taking a warm bath.

2. Reflect: Take a few moments to reflect on your day. Acknowledge your accomplishments and express gratitude for the good things that happened.

3. Prepare for Tomorrow: Lay out your clothes for the next day, pack your bag, or make a to-do list to set yourself up for success in the morning.

4. Mindful Eating: Avoid heavy meals or caffeine close to bedtime. Opt for a light snack if you're hungry, but avoid anything that might disrupt your sleep.

5. Relaxation Techniques: Practice relaxation techniques like deep breathing or progressive muscle relaxation to help your body and mind unwind.

6. Bedtime Routine: Establish a consistent bedtime routine to signal to your body that it's time to sleep. This could include brushing your teeth, dimming the lights, and reading a book. Quality Sleep Environment: Create a comfortable sleep environment by keeping your bedroom cool, dark, and quiet. Invest in a comfortable mattress and pillows to support restful sleep.

By following these step-by-step processes for creating successful morning and evening routines, you can set yourself up for a day filled with energy, productivity, and well-being, while also ensuring a restful night's sleep.

MORNING/NIGHT ROUTINE

USE THIS FORM TO WRITE ANY ROUTINE IDEAS

Morning and evening routines intertwine with the third eye chakra in profound ways. By starting the day with practices like meditation or journaling, you awaken intuition and clarity, fostering a deeper sense of awareness. Reflecting on your day in the evening nurtures self-awareness and insight, encouraging trust in your inner wisdom. Dreamwork during bedtime can tap into subconscious messages, reinforcing intuitive guidance. Throughout the day, mindfulness practices sustain the activation of the third eye chakra, enhancing perception and spiritual insight. These routines collectively support a balanced and heightened awareness, enriching daily experiences with clarity and intuition.

ROUTINES

FILL OUT AFTER YOU CREATE YOUR ROUTINES

Today I am grateful for:

My Top 3 Goals

Schedule

To Do List

- [ ]
- [ ]
- [ ]
- [ ]
- [ ]
- [ ]
- [ ]
- [ ]
- [ ]

How was my salt bath?

Discover Your Calling

ROUTINES-DAY THREE

As a Taurus, I'm naturally a creature of habit. Over time, though, I've learned that flexibility can be just as grounding as routine. Rather than sticking to a strict schedule, I embrace freedom in how I get things done. My morning routine allows this flow, with each task having a minimum, average, and above-average version. As long as I hit the minimum, I celebrate my consistency and discipline in self-care.

Exercise, for instance, is a non-negotiable part of my mornings. My bare minimum? A simple stretch to wake up my body. The average? A 30-minute walk to get my blood flowing. And on days I feel extra motivated, I go all in with a full hour workout, weights included. No matter which version I choose, I honor the effort and acknowledge that I'm prioritizing myself and keeping my routine alive.

This approach keeps me accountable without piling on the pressure. I've come to value that every effort, at any level, counts. Embracing this flexibility has helped me feel more balanced, allowing me to care for myself in a way that feels authentic and sustainable.

DAY FOUR
FOOD

The connection between food and the throat chakra lies in how nourishment supports our physical health and our ability to communicate and express ourselves authentically. Just as the throat chakra serves as the center of communication, food nourishes our bodies, providing the energy and vitality needed to articulate thoughts and feelings clearly. Choosing foods that soothe and support the throat, such as herbal teas, fruits, and hydrating foods, can promote vocal health and ease of expression.

Our bodies thank us when we eat a balanced diet with lots of good stuff like fruits, veggies, and lean proteins. We get the energy we need, our immune systems stay strong, and our organs function well.

Boosting our mood: Believe it or not, what we eat can totally affect how we feel. Foods rich in omega-3s, B vitamins, and antioxidants can boost our brains, helping us feel happier and more focused.

What we eat can totally affect our skin! Loading up on nutrient-rich foods like colorful fruits and veggies, healthy fats, and lean proteins gives our skin the vitamins and antioxidants it needs to stay healthy, elastic, and looking its best.

RECOMMENDATION

WRITE OUT YOUR IDEAL MEAL PLAN THAT PROMOTES OPTIMAL HEALTH AND WELL-BEING. GO GROCERY SHOPPING AND COOK. BUDGET WISELY.

MAKING MEAL PLANS - 20 ITEMS/15 MEALS

Here are 20 grocery items to create breakfast, lunch, and dinner for five days:

1. Eggs
2. Whole wheat bread
3. Chicken breast
4. Ground beef
5. Salmon fillets
6. Quinoa
7. Brown rice
8. Spaghetti
9. Greek yogurt
10. Mixed vegetables (frozen or fresh)
11. Spinach
12. Tomatoes
13. Avocado
14. Carrots
15. Bell peppers
16. Onions
17. Cucumber
18. Lettuce (romaine)
19. Cheddar cheese
20. Marinara sauce

Here's a five-day meal plan using the 20 grocery items listed:

Day 1:

Breakfast: Scrambled eggs with spinach

Lunch: Chicken and vegetable stir-fry with brown rice

Dinner: Baked salmon with roasted vegetables (bell peppers, carrots, onions)

Day 2:

Breakfast: Avocado toast with sliced tomatoes

Lunch: Ground beef taco salad with lettuce, tomatoes, cheddar cheese, and avocado

Dinner: Spaghetti with marinara sauce and a side salad (lettuce, cucumber)

Day 3:

Breakfast: Greek yogurt topped with mixed berries and granola

Lunch: Quinoa salad with mixed vegetables (carrots, bell peppers, cucumber)

Dinner: Chicken and vegetable stir-fry with brown rice

Day 4:

Breakfast: Scrambled eggs with spinach and cheddar cheese

Lunch: Salmon salad with mixed greens, tomatoes, and avocado

Dinner: Ground beef tacos with lettuce, tomatoes, and cheddar cheese

Day 5:

Breakfast: Omelette with spinach, tomatoes, and cheddar cheese

Lunch: Chicken Caesar salad with romaine lettuce, grilled chicken breast, and Caesar dressing

Dinner: Baked salmon with roasted vegetables (bell peppers, carrots, onions)

MEAL PLAN

Monday:

Monday:

Monday:

Monday:

Monday:

Monday:

Monday:

Discover Your Calling

FOOD

FILL OUT AFTER CREATING GROCERY LIST

Schedule   My Top 3 Goals

_____

_____

_____

Schedule   To Do List

☐ _____
☐ _____
☐ _____
☐ _____
☐ _____
☐ _____
☐ _____
☐ _____
☐ _____

How do I feel about the items on my grocery list, and how simple was it for me to create it?

_____

_____

_____

_____

_____

FOOD-DAY FOUR

Right now, I'm focused on making healthier food choices. I've started exploring new recipes, planning meals ahead, and learning how to use the same ingredients across different dishes to keep costs down. Portion control is key for me since I'm a true foodie at heart.

This is also a time of experimenting with food. Through this challenge, I've ventured into cooking different cultural cuisines, crafted my own recipes, and rediscovered my love for cooking. When I get it right, I only cook twice a week, moving smoothly from grocery prep to a spotless kitchen in just three hours. This routine brings a satisfying rhythm to my week, balancing enjoyment with mindfulness.

Root Vegetable Sancocho

Prepping time: 15 min   Cooking time: 45 min

Ingredients

1 carrot, chopped

1 small yellow onion

1 parsnip, chopped

1 Not-Chik'n Bouillon cube

1 sweet potato, chopped

1 plantain, peeled and sliced into 1/2 inch slices

15.25 oz can of sweet corn   Brown rice

Salt

Olive oil

Pepper

2 tsp Spicy Special Seasoning (similar to Alamo Seasoning)

Arrange a rack in the middle of the oven and heat the oven to 425°F.

1. Peel the vegetables, then cut them into rough 1 inch chunks. Cut one small yellow onion into 1/2 inch chunks. Place the root vegetables on a baking sheet. Drizzle with olive oil, sprinkle with salt and pepper and toss to evenly coat. Spread out in an even layer.

2. Roast for 30 minutes. Remove the baking sheet from the oven.

3. Heat olive oil in a medium saucepan over medium high heat. Add root vegetables and onion and cook until vegetables begin to soften, 3 to 5 minutes. Add bouillon cube, plantains, and spicy special seasoning and stir to combine. Add 4 cups of water and bring to a boil. Reduce heat to a simmer and cook until plantains are tender, 30 to 45 minutes.

4. While the soup simmers, make your brown rice. For every 1 cup of rice, use 1 1/2 cups water.

5. Finally heat a medium nonstick skillet over medium high heat add sweet corn, and 1 teaspoon olive oil to the skillet and cook, stirring occasionally, for 4 to 8 minutes.

6. Place rice in a bowl ladle the soup around the rice and top with the corn. Bon appétit.

DAY FIVE
TOXICITY

The connection between root chakra toxicity and its impact on our overall well-being is multifaceted. The root chakra, situated at the base of the spine, governs our sense of safety, security, and stability in the world. When this chakra becomes imbalanced or blocked, it can manifest as toxicity in various aspects of our lives.

Root chakra toxicity often stems from feelings of fear, insecurity, and instability. This toxicity may arise from past traumas, financial worries, or a lack of a supportive social network. When the root chakra is overwhelmed by these negative energies, it can lead to a range of physical, emotional, and psychological symptoms.

Physically, root chakra toxicity may manifest as issues such as lower back pain, digestive problems, or immune system imbalances. Emotionally, it can result in feelings of anxiety, depression, or a pervasive sense of unease. Psychologically, root chakra toxicity may manifest as an inability to trust others, chronic stress, or difficulty in feeling grounded and present in the moment.

Furthermore, root chakra toxicity can impact our relationships, career, and overall sense of fulfillment in life. It may lead to patterns of self-sabotage, avoidance of change or risk, and a constant seeking of external validation or security.

RECOMMENDATION

WHAT TOXIC THOUGHTS AND TRAITS DO I NEED TO IDENTIFY, ADDRESS, AND ACTIVELY WORK ON CHANGING FOR PERSONAL GROWTH AND WELL-BEING?

ENGAGING IN SHADOW WORK

Here's a sample five-step plan to address and change toxic behavior:

1. Recognize and Acknowledge: The first step is to recognize and acknowledge the toxic behavior. Reflect on your actions and their impact on yourself and others. Take ownership of your behavior without blaming others or making excuses.

2. Understand Triggers and Patterns: Explore the triggers and underlying patterns that contribute to the toxic behavior. Identify situations, emotions, or thoughts that often lead to the behavior. Understanding these triggers can help you develop strategies to manage them more effectively.

3. Seek Support and Accountability: Reach out to trusted friends, family members, or professionals for support and accountability. Share your intention to change and ask for feedback and encouragement along the way. Consider joining a support group or seeking therapy if necessary.

4. Develop Healthy Coping Mechanisms: Replace toxic behavior with healthier coping mechanisms. Practice self-care activities such as exercise, mindfulness, or hobbies that promote relaxation and positive emotions. Learn and practice effective communication skills to express yourself assertively and constructively.

5. Monitor Progress and Adjust: Regularly monitor your progress and be willing to adjust your approach as needed. Celebrate small victories and milestones along the way, but also be patient with

yourself during setbacks. Stay committed to your goal of change and remember that personal growth is a journey.

By following this five-step plan, you can address and change toxic behavior, fostering healthier relationships and a more fulfilling life.

Shadow work is the process of exploring and integrating the unconscious aspects of oneself, including negative traits and suppressed emotions, to promote self-awareness and personal growth. Engaging in shadow work can be a powerful tool for addressing and transforming toxic behavior. By delving into the depths of our subconscious and uncovering hidden beliefs, fears, and patterns, we can shine a light on the aspects of ourselves that contribute to toxicity. The "I WANT" deck can support this process by providing prompts and questions that encourage self-reflection and exploration. Through shadow work, we confront the parts of ourselves that we may have been avoiding or denying, allowing us to acknowledge and integrate them with compassion and understanding. By facing our shadows head-on, we gain insight into the root causes of our toxic behavior and empower ourselves to make meaningful changes towards healing and growth.

TOXIC TRAITS ASSESSMENT

Quiz: Are You Displaying Toxic Traits?

**Do you often find yourself criticizing or belittling others, either openly or behind their backs?

Yes   No

Sometimes

**When faced with conflict or disagreement, do you tend to become defensive or dismissive rather than open to discussion and compromise?

Yes   No

Sometimes

**Do you frequently prioritize your own needs and desires over the well-being and feelings of others?

Yes   No

Sometimes

**Do you often manipulate or guilt-trip others to get what you want, rather than communicating your needs directly?

Yes   No

Sometimes

**Are you prone to jealousy or resentment towards others'

successes or happiness?

Yes   No

Sometimes

**Do you struggle to take responsibility for your actions and tend to blame others or external circumstances instead?

Yes   No

Sometimes

**Do you find yourself engaging in gossip or spreading rumors about others?

Yes   No

Sometimes

Results:

If you answered "Yes" to most questions, you may be displaying toxic traits that could harm your relationships and well-being.

If you answered "Sometimes" to some questions, consider reflecting on these behaviors and how they may impact yourself and those around you.

If you answered "No" to most questions, you demonstrate healthy behaviors that contribute to positive and respectful relationships.

TOXICITY

FILL OUT AFTER TAKING TOXICITY ASSESSMENT

Today I am grateful for:

My Top 3 Goals

Schedule

To Do List

- [ ]
- [ ]
- [ ]
- [ ]
- [ ]
- [ ]
- [ ]
- [ ]
- [ ]

Did I address my toxicity today? How did it make me feel?

Discover Your Calling

TOXICITY-DAY FIVE

After several days of building myself up, it's time to confront my vices, challenges, and fears. This is always the hardest part of the week for me during this experiment. I have to face the aspects of myself that I dislike or feel uneasy about.

Writing a list of flaws isn't easy, so I often turn to my I WANT deck for support. This time, I drew the card UNEMOTIONAL, and it became clear that it was time to open up and allow myself to be vulnerable again. I had learned the boundaries I needed, communicated them clearly, and put in the healing work. Now, it felt safe to show love again.

I realize that sometimes, toxic traits emerge from a place of protection rather than malice. I grow and heal by pushing past the surface—beyond the label or habit—and understanding why these traits exist. It's a reminder that I don't have to be perfect. My flaws aren't definitive; they hold the potential to refine me.

I've learned to embrace my darker qualities with the same acceptance I give my strengths. Acknowledging both light and dark within myself has become essential. In fact, I feel more connected to those who openly face their own flaws and fears than to those who shy away from them. True growth lies in accepting and understanding both sides of who we are.

DAY SIX
VALUES

Boundaries and values are essential elements in preserving self-care. Here's why they are important:

Protection of well-being: Values establish limits and define what is acceptable and unacceptable in our interactions, relationships, and experiences.

Respect for oneself: When we establish and uphold boundaries, we send a message to ourselves and others that our needs, values, and personal space matter.

Alignment with personal values: Self-care is deeply connected to our personal values. For example, if our value is to prioritize quality time with loved ones, we must establish boundaries around work hours or device usage to ensure dedicated time for nurturing relationships.

Energy preservation: Boundaries and values help us conserve energy and prevent burnout. By saying no to commitments or interactions that deplete our energy or go against our values, we create space for self-care activities and experiences that replenish and recharge us.

Stress reduction: When we have clear boundaries, we minimize the likelihood of overextending ourselves, taking on excessive responsibilities, or being constantly available to others.

RECOMMENDATION

PICK THE TWO VALUES YOU HOLD MOST IMPORTANT FROM THE LIST BELOW OR PICK YOUR OWN. COMMIT TO THEM..

CREATING A FIRM VALUE SYSTEM

Here's a five-step sample plan to figure out what your value system may be:

1. Self-Reflection: Take time to reflect on your beliefs, principles, and priorities. Consider moments in your life when you felt fulfilled, proud, or aligned with your values. Journaling or meditation can help you explore your thoughts and feelings more deeply.

2. Identify Core Values: Identify the core values that resonate most strongly with you. These are the principles that guide your decisions, actions, and interactions with others. Common values include integrity, compassion, honesty, authenticity, and resilience.

3. Assess Priorities: Consider what is most important to you in various areas of your life, such as relationships, career, health, and personal development. Rank your priorities and determine how they align with your core values.

4. Seek Feedback: Seek feedback from trusted friends, family members, or mentors about what they perceive to be your values. Their perspectives can offer valuable insights and help you gain clarity about your own beliefs and priorities.

5. Reflect on Actions: Reflect on your actions and behaviors to see if they align with your identified values. Notice instances when you feel proud or fulfilled, as well as moments of discomfort or conflict. Use these experiences to refine and clarify your understanding of your value system.

By following this five-step plan, you can gain a deeper

understanding of your value system and use it as a guiding force in your life decisions and actions.

Values are the deeply-held beliefs, principles, and priorities that guide individuals' thoughts, decisions, and actions, shaping their identity and influencing their behavior.

Understanding and aligning with your value system can have a profound impact on your self-esteem and contribute to addressing toxic behavior. The "1 AM" deck provides valuable support in this process by prompting self-reflection and exploration of personal values. By clarifying your values and honoring them in your actions and relationships, you cultivate a sense of self-worth and authenticity. This strengthens your self-esteem, making you less likely to engage in toxic behavior driven by insecurity or a lack of self-awareness. When you prioritize values such as respect, integrity, and empathy, you naturally gravitate towards healthier interactions and choices, fostering positive relationships and personal growth. Through this journey of self-discovery and alignment with your values, you empower yourself to break free from toxic patterns and live a more fulfilling and authentic life.

SENDING LIGHT AND LOVE

Our personal value system is deeply intertwined with the heart chakra, the center of love, compassion, and empathy. When we live in alignment with our values, we honor our true essence and cultivate a deep sense of connection with ourselves and others. Just as the heart chakra governs our ability to give and receive love unconditionally, our values guide us in forming meaningful relationships and fostering a sense of unity and harmony in the world.

By embracing values such as kindness, forgiveness, and generosity, we open our hearts to the beauty and diversity of human experience. These values encourage us to treat ourselves and others with compassion and understanding, fostering a sense of empathy and acceptance. Similarly, when we act in accordance with our values, we contribute to the collective well-being, creating a ripple effect of love and positivity that extends far beyond ourselves.

Conversely, when we neglect or betray our values, we may experience feelings of disconnect, resentment, or emotional imbalance. This disconnect can manifest as blockages in the heart chakra, leading to difficulties in forming authentic connections and experiencing deep, meaningful relationships.

By honoring our personal value system and living in alignment with the principles of the heart chakra, we nurture a profound sense of love and connection within ourselves and with the world around us. In doing so, we open ourselves to the transformative power of love, fostering healing, growth, and fulfillment in our lives.

Sample list of values:

Honesty	Generosity	Loyalty
Integrity	Empathy	Courage
Respect	Forgiveness	Open-mindedness
Compassion	Authenticity	Optimism
Responsibility	Courage	Patience
Gratitude	Perseverance	Fairness
Kindness	Humility	Accepting

VALUE

FILL OUT AFTER ASSESSING MY VALUE SYSTEMT

Schedule   My Top 3 Goals

Schedule   To Do List

☐
☐
☐
☐
☐
☐
☐
☐
☐

What are my top 2 values and why?

Discover Your Calling

VALUES-DAY SIX

There was a time when I didn't think too deeply about my own qualities. I'd use words like wise or funny to describe myself—safe choices that didn't really evoke anything profound.

One day, I asked a friend what two words she'd choose to describe me. She paused thoughtfully before saying, "vivacious and deep." Those words landed with an unexpected weight; they resonated so strongly that I immediately thanked her and promised I'd adopt them as my own.

This experience taught me something vital: the words I use to describe myself should stir something within me. When I started owning vivacious and deep, I felt a shift—I stood a little taller, felt more grounded, and allowed my energy to take up space in a way it hadn't before.

That day, I spent hours exploring words that weren't just fun or colorful but meaningful. I realized that if I ever choose new words in the future, I want to expand beyond the familiar; limiting my language limits how I view myself. As someone who values language deeply, finding words that truly reflect who I am—not just words that fit the moment—has become an essential part of self-discovery.

DAY SEVEN
FITNESS

Exercise and fitness play a vital role in the importance of self-care. Here's why they are significant:

Physical well-being: Physical activity helps improve cardiovascular health, strengthen muscles and bones, enhance flexibility and mobility, and support weight management. Regular exercise also reduces the risk of chronic diseases such as heart disease, diabetes, and certain types of cancer.

Mental health benefits: Exercise has a powerful impact on our mental health. Physical activity stimulates the release of endorphins, often called "feel-good" hormones, which can improve mood and reduce symptoms of stress, anxiety, and depression.

Stress reduction: Physical activity helps reduce the levels of stress hormones like cortisol and adrenaline in our bodies. Engaging in exercise can be a form of active relaxation, allowing us to focus our minds on the activity and temporarily set aside stressors.

Self-confidence and body image: Exercise can improve self-confidence and body image. Physical activity can improve physical appearance, fitness levels, and overall health. Engaging in exercise and achieving fitness goals can boost self-esteem, enhance body positivity, and foster a more positive relationship with our bodies.

RECOMMENDATION

PICK THE TWO VALUES YOU HOLD MOST IMPORTANT FROM THE LIST BELOW OR PICK YOUR OWN. COMMIT TO THEM..

FITNESS SCHEDULE FIT FOR ME

When creating a fitness schedule and aiming to stick to it, consider the following step-by-step approach:

1. Set Clear Goals: Define specific and achievable fitness goals, whether it's weight loss, muscle gain, improved endurance, or overall health and well-being.

2. Assess Your Current Fitness Level: Evaluate your current fitness level, including strengths, weaknesses, and any limitations or health concerns that may impact your exercise routine.

3. Choose Activities You Enjoy: Select exercises and activities that you genuinely enjoy and look forward to, as this increases the likelihood of sticking to your fitness schedule long-term.

4. Create a Realistic Schedule: Develop a realistic fitness schedule that fits into your daily routine and allows for consistency. Consider factors such as time of day, duration of workouts, and frequency of exercise sessions.

5. Include Variety: Incorporate a variety of exercises and activities into your fitness schedule to target different muscle groups, prevent boredom, and reduce the risk of overuse injuries.

6. Progress Gradually: Start slowly and gradually increase the intensity, duration, and frequency of your workouts as your fitness level improves. Listen to your body and avoid pushing yourself too hard, especially if you're new to exercise.

7. Track Your Progress: Keep track of your workouts, progress

towards your goals, and any changes in your fitness level. This can help you stay motivated and make adjustments to your fitness schedule as needed.

8. Stay Flexible: Be flexible and adaptable with your fitness schedule, especially when life gets busy or unexpected events arise. Find alternative ways to stay active and prioritize consistency over perfection.

9. Find Support: Surround yourself with a supportive network of friends, family members, or fitness buddies who can encourage and motivate you along your fitness journey.

10. Celebrate Achievements: Celebrate your achievements and milestones along the way, whether it's reaching a new personal best, completing a challenging workout, or sticking to your fitness schedule consistently.

By following these steps and staying committed to your fitness goals, you can create a sustainable fitness schedule and increase your chances of sticking to it for the long haul.

FIT MESS

Fitness and the solar plexus chakra are intricately connected through their shared emphasis on personal power, self-discipline, and confidence. Just as the solar plexus chakra serves as the energetic center of willpower and self-esteem, fitness practices empower us to cultivate strength, resilience, and a sense of mastery over our physical bodies.

Regular exercise and fitness routines challenge us to push past our perceived limits, tapping into our inner reservoirs of determination and resilience. Setting and achieving fitness goals bolsters our self-confidence and self-esteem, affirming our capabilities and potential. This process of self-improvement fosters a deep sense of personal power, aligning with the energy of the solar plexus chakra and empowering us to take decisive action in pursuit of our aspirations.

Furthermore, fitness practices promote holistic well-being, encompassing physical, mental, and emotional dimensions of health. By caring for our bodies through exercise, we nourish the energetic flow within the solar plexus chakra, promoting balance and vitality on both a physical and energetic level. This harmonious alignment of body and spirit enhances our overall sense of well-being, instilling a profound sense of confidence, courage, and inner strength.

Conversely, neglecting our physical health can lead to imbalances in the solar plexus chakra, manifesting as feelings of insecurity, indecision, or a lack of self-worth. By prioritizing fitness and wellness practices, we honor the sacred connection between our physical bodies and our inner sense of power and vitality, fostering a deeper alignment with the transformative energy of the solar plexus chakra.

Here's a short fitness routine you can try:

1. **Warm-up (5 minutes):**

Jog in place or jump rope for 1 minute

Arm circles (20 seconds forward, 20 seconds backward)

Bodyweight squats (10 reps)

Lunges (10 reps each leg)

Arm swings (10 reps each side)

2. **Circuit (15 minutes):**

Push-ups (10 reps)

Bodyweight squats (15 reps)

Mountain climbers (20 reps)

Plank hold (30 seconds)

Bicycle crunches (15 reps each side)

Jumping jacks (30 seconds)

Rest for 1 minute, then repeat the circuit 2 more times

3. **Cool-down and stretching (5 minutes):**

Deep breathing and relaxation (2 minutes)

Hamstring stretch (30 seconds each leg)

Quadriceps stretch (30 seconds each leg)

Shoulder stretch (30 seconds each arm)

Chest opener stretch (30 seconds)

FITNESS

FILL OUT AFTER CREATING YOUR FITNESS SCHEDULE

Today I am grateful for:

My Top 3 Goals

Schedule

To Do List
- [ ]
- [ ]
- [ ]
- [ ]
- [ ]
- [ ]
- [ ]
- [ ]
- [ ]

Did I create a fitness schedule?

Discover Your Calling

FITNESS-DAY SEVEN

Fitness has always been a tricky path for me. I love non-traditional exercise but, like most people, still want those traditional results—toned arms, a six-pack, the works.

Days like this test me. Traditional workouts aren't my favorite, even though they're the quickest way to see physical changes. I'd rather be swimming, walking, or hiking, but I've invested in weights and yoga mats to bring that challenge home. This part of my routine is always the hardest, but a mantra keeps echoing in my mind: consistency, discipline, safety. I remind myself that I'm doing this for me. When I'm fit, I feel better, look better, and that alone makes the effort worthwhile.

Today, I did the bare minimum—just 30 minutes. I've learned that if I don't get it done first thing in the morning, it won't happen at all. So, at 5:00 a.m., I get up. By 5:30 a.m., I'm stretching, and by 7:00 a.m., I'm done, savoring my coffee and grateful for pushing through what sometimes feels like torture. Yet I know, in the end, it's worth every bit.

PERSONAL ACCOUNTABILITY

Identify and prioritize the top internal or external factors I would like to address.

Habit										
1	2	3	4	5	6	7	8	9	10	11
12	13	14	15	16	17	18	19	20	21	22
23	24	25	26	27	28	29	30	31		

Habit										
1	2	3	4	5	6	7	8	9	10	11
12	13	14	15	16	17	18	19	20	21	22
23	24	25	26	27	28	29	30	31		

Habit										
1	2	3	4	5	6	7	8	9	10	11
12	13	14	15	16	17	18	19	20	21	22
23	24	25	26	27	28	29	30	31		

Habit										
1	2	3	4	5	6	7	8	9	10	11
12	13	14	15	16	17	18	19	20	21	22
23	24	25	26	27	28	29	30	31		

Habit										
1	2	3	4	5	6	7	8	9	10	11
12	13	14	15	16	17	18	19	20	21	22
23	24	25	26	27	28	29	30	31		

Habit										
1	2	3	4	5	6	7	8	9	10	11
12	13	14	15	16	17	18	19	20	21	22
23	24	25	26	27	28	29	30	31		

PERSONAL ACCOUNTABILITY

Identify and prioritize the top internal or external factors I would like to address.

Habit:	Exercise for 30 minutes a day										
~~1~~	~~2~~	~~3~~	~~4~~	~~5~~	~~6~~	~~7~~	8	9	10	11	
12	13	14	15	16	17	18	19	20	21	22	
23	24	25	26	27	28	29	30	31			

Habit:	Meditate for 2 minutes a day										
~~1~~	~~2~~	~~3~~	~~4~~	~~5~~	~~6~~	~~7~~	8	9	10	11	
12	13	14	15	16	17	18	19	20	21	22	
23	24	25	26	27	28	29	30	31			

Habit:	Declutter personal space										
~~1~~	~~2~~	~~3~~	~~4~~	~~5~~	~~6~~	~~7~~	8	9	10	11	
12	13	14	15	16	17	18	19	20	21	22	
23	24	25	26	27	28	29	30	31			

Habit:	Wear light colors. (Starts Day 2)										
1	~~2~~	~~3~~	~~4~~	~~5~~	~~6~~	~~7~~	~~8~~	9	10	11	
12	13	14	15	16	17	18	19	20	21	22	
23	24	25	26	27	28	29	30	31			

Habit:	Incorporate morning and evening routine elements. (Starts Day 3)										
1	2	~~3~~	~~4~~	~~5~~	~~6~~	~~7~~	~~8~~	~~9~~	10	11	
12	13	14	15	16	17	18	19	20	21	22	
23	24	25	26	27	28	29	30	31			

Habit:	Focus on fitness. (Starts on Day 7 for 7 days)										
1	2	3	4	5	6	~~7~~	~~8~~	~~9~~	~~10~~	~~11~~	
~~12~~	~~13~~	14	15	16	17	18	19	20	21	22	
23	24	25	26	27	28	29	30	31			

www.liveintruthspace.com

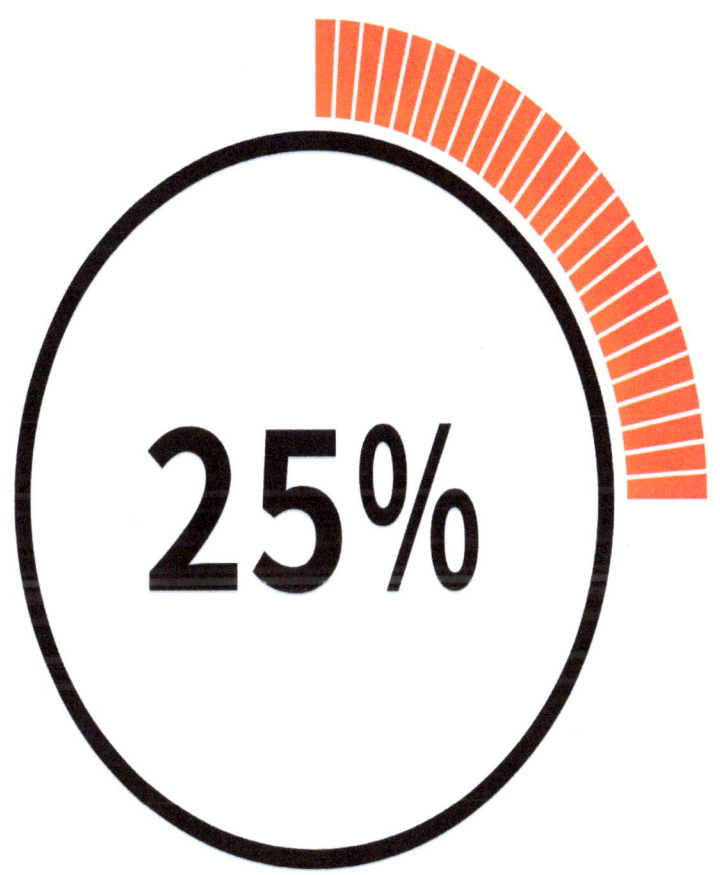

MODULE 3
INTUITION

Congratulations, and keep going! Take another salt bath, meal prep, and keep on exercising! Now, we have shifted to working on trust. You must trust yourself more than anyone else. Who knows you better than you do? No one.

GET INTO IT
TO GET INTUIT.

WHY THIS PROCESS?

Every day, I talk to people who feel like their lives are in transition; they're not sure where they're going and lost. This is happening globally, and I hope to shed light on why knowing and pursuing purpose are essential to self-love, love for others, and mental clarity.

This course is broken down into seven lessons, followed by intuitive training tips and tricks for the oracle decks. You only have to pick one exercise from each list to try that day. This is the only direction you have this week. It's time to trust yourself. This section is a guide to YOUR best self. As the lessons progress, you begin to see all the ways you can train your brain to trust itself. The biggest thing to learn is to trust the process because it works when you do the work.

95 % of blockages are unconscious, so by making ourselves more aware of subconscious thoughts, which these lessons do, we train ourselves to find pockets of peace in the panic to make sound choices.

When I learn who I am, I am able to teach people how to treat me. I create a deeper understanding of who I am.

MY STORY

Spirituality isn't something that I happily walked into. I am not a religious person, however experiencing all the crazy things that happened to me from childhood to now, I had to understand and acknowledge that a higher power was guiding and helping me, so now it was time to help myself.

No matter how others tried to break me, I trusted that I was on my right path. I kept telling myself, the harder the tests, the greater the reward.

I began making my first oracle deck, I AM, in 2020. I was struggling with my health and happiness. I was in a toxic relationship, acting on a TV show, in the process of buying my first house and covid was coviding. I was looking for light and peace.

At this time, I also wrote my third book, I'd Rather Be Happy and Pee. It was all about dealing with shadow work, the dark qualities and elements surrounding my energy and those around me. Mastering my intuition has given me peace.

I am a Healer, an Intuitive. I promise you, even if you think I don't know, I know, yet I give grace. I learned to trust what I feel and think first instead of relying on outside resources to confirm. It's a powerful place to be and I hope you thrive in this new venture of trusting your ability to discern what is best for you and rid yourself of people, places, and things that threaten that peace. Welcome to this course!

Maya Lynne

WHAT IS INTUITION?

ETYMOLOGY OF INTUITION

Plato had a take on intuition in his Republic. He thought of it as our mind's way of grasping the real deal about reality. In works like Meno and Phaedo, he called it a sort of built-in knowledge in our "soul of eternity." Take math, for example. Plato figured we don't reason our way to those truths; they're more like déjà vu moments, where we're tapping into what's already in us. Some folks even call this idea "anamnesis." Plato's brainy pals, the Neoplatonists, kept digging into this intuition stuff after him.

THE MATRIX

In "The Matrix," the protagonist, Neo, is constantly faced with the choice of blindly accepting the reality presented to him or trusting his intuitive sense that something is off or wrong. This theme is symbolized by the iconic red pill/blue pill choice, where Neo's decision hinges on his gut feeling rather than tangible evidence.

As Neo navigates the simulated reality, his journey becomes a metaphor for the importance of discernment. The Matrix challenges us to question our surroundings and not merely accept them at face value. Neo's journey teaches us to listen to our own inner voice, even when the external world seems convincing.

The character of the Oracle, a guide within the Matrix, plays a crucial role in emphasizing the reliance on intuition. Her mysterious and mystifying counsel encourages Neo to trust his instincts and make choices based on a deeper understanding of himself rather than external influences.

Reality is not always what it seems and discernment, coupled with intuitive trust, is key to unveiling hidden truths. "The Matrix" ultimately champions the empowerment that comes from tapping into one's inner wisdom, challenging the status quo, and navigating a path guided by personal intuition.

I hope this explanation helped you.

WHY THIS WORKS?

Career Decisions:

Strengthening intuition can aid in making career decisions. For instance, when choosing between job opportunities, your intuition might guide you toward the option that aligns better with your values and long-term goals, even if it doesn't seem like the most logical choice on the surface.

Relationships:

Intuition is crucial in matters of the heart. Strengthening it can help you navigate relationships, whether it's discerning the authenticity of new connections or understanding when it's time to nurture or let go of existing ones. Your intuition often senses subtle cues that may not be immediately evident.

Health and Well-being:

Paying attention to your intuition can contribute to better health decisions. It might guide you in choosing the right exercise routine, identifying when your body needs rest, or even guiding you towards certain foods that make you feel more energized and nourished.

Creativity and Innovation:

Strengthening intuition fosters creativity. It allows you to trust your instincts in the creative process, whether you're an artist, writer, or problem solver. Intuition often leads to innovative ideas and solutions that may not emerge through purely analytical thinking.

Life Transitions:

During major life transitions, such as moving to a new city or considering a career change, intuition can offer valuable insights. It helps you tap into your inner desires, fears, and aspirations, guiding you toward choices that resonate with your authentic self.

Financial Decision-Making:

Intuition can play a role in financial decisions. Strengthening it may help you sense when to invest, save, or spend. It often serves as an additional layer of guidance beyond purely analytical approaches to financial planning.

Conflict Resolution:

Intuition aids in interpersonal dynamics and conflict resolution. It can help you sense the underlying emotions and intentions of others, fostering empathy and improving communication skills in various relationships.

Personal Growth and Fulfillment:

Strengthening intuition contributes to personal growth and fulfillment. It guides you in understanding your passions, purpose, and the paths that align with your authentic self, leading to a more satisfying and meaningful life journey.

MINDFULNESS-DAY 8

Pick one exercise from the list to try today.

Consistent Routine:

Establish a regular meditation routine by allocating a specific time each day.

Consistency helps build a habit and deepens the benefits over time.

Mindful Breathing:

Focus on your breath to anchor yourself in the present moment.

Experiment with different breathing techniques, such as deep belly breathing or counting breaths.

Guided Meditations:

Use guided meditation sessions, either through apps, podcasts, or live classes.

Guided sessions can provide structure and help you explore different aspects of mindfulness.

EXTRAS

Mindful Walking:

Take short mindful walks, paying attention to each step and your surroundings.

This can be a refreshing alternative to seated meditation.

Mindfulness Apps:

Explore mindfulness and meditation apps that offer a variety of practices.

Apps often provide timers, reminders, and progress tracking.

Create a Sacred Space:

Designate a quiet and comfortable space for meditation.

Personalize it with calming elements like cushions, candles, or meaningful objects.

Mindful Eating:

Practice mindfulness during meals by savoring each bite and paying attention to flavors, textures, and smells.

This can deepen your overall awareness.

Be gentle with yourself if your mind wanders during meditation. Embrace the practice without judgment, and gently guide your focus back to the present.

MINDFULNESS AND INTUITION

Mindfulness is a powerful practice for increasing and nurturing intuitive thinking. By cultivating present-moment awareness and non-judgmental observation of our thoughts, emotions, and sensations, mindfulness allows us to quiet the noise of the mind and access our intuitive wisdom more readily. Through mindfulness meditation, breathwork, or mindful movement practices such as yoga, we learn to tune into the subtle cues and signals of our intuition with greater clarity and sensitivity.

When we approach life with a mindful attitude, we become more attuned to the present moment, allowing us to notice the subtle nuances and insights that arise from our intuition. By slowing down and paying attention to our inner experiences without attachment or resistance, we create space for intuitive thoughts and impulses to emerge naturally.

Moreover, mindfulness helps us develop greater discernment and clarity in distinguishing between our intuition and other mental chatter or conditioning. By cultivating a non-reactive and curious attitude towards our thoughts and emotions, we can discern the wisdom of our intuition from the noise of fear, doubt, or past conditioning.

In essence, mindfulness creates the fertile ground upon which intuitive thinking can flourish. By anchoring ourselves in the present moment and cultivating a receptive mindset, we open ourselves up to the deeper wisdom and insight that lie within us, leading to more informed decisions, greater creativity, and a deeper sense of connection to ourselves and the world around us.

MEDITATION 7-DAY CHALLENGE

Can I commit to 5 minutes of meditation a day?

Consistency. Discipline. Safety.

1 _____

2 _____

3 _____

4 _____

5 _____

6 _____

7 _____

MINDFULNESS FOLLOW UP REFLECTION

Which mindfulness tip did I pick and why?

_____

_____

_____

Did I take 5 minutes to center myself with a quick meditation?

_____

_____

_____

How am I continuing my self-care routine as I go through this course?

_____

_____

_____

Do I have additional thoughts?

_____

_____

_____

MINDFULNESS-DAY 8

Mindfulness has been a journey, to say the least. When I first committed to sitting still for just five minutes each day, I assumed it would be simple—but I quickly learned otherwise. My mind would wander almost instantly, filled with thoughts of tasks, projects, or how I could improve something. Turning off my brain felt nearly impossible.

In those early days, I spent more time wrestling with my thoughts than finding peace. But I stayed with it, day after day. Slowly, I began to understand that mindfulness isn't about silencing the mind; it's about allowing thoughts to come and go without feeling the need to act on them. Over time, those five minutes shifted from a struggle to a grounding part of my day.

Now, those five minutes feel like a gift—a chance to reset, clear my head, and simply be. It wasn't easy at the start, but as I practiced, it became easier to give myself this small space. This journey has taught me that mindfulness is a process, one that grows lighter with time and patience.

TRUST-DAY 9

Pick one exercise from the list to try today.

10 Ways You Know You Are Trusting Yourself

Instinctual Decision-Making:

Follow-up Question: How often do you find yourself making decisions based on your initial instincts without overthinking?

Embracing Authenticity:

Follow-up Question: In what situations are you most comfortable being your authentic self?

Inner Peace and Calm:

Follow-up Question: How often do you experience a sense of calm and inner peace in your daily life?

Setting Boundaries:

Follow-up Question: Are you able to establish and maintain healthy boundaries in your relationships and activities?

Confidence in Choices:

Follow-up Question: How confident do you feel in the choices you make, even when they deviate from external expectations?

Positive Self-Talk:

Follow-up Question: What is the nature of your internal dialogue?

How often do you practice positive self-talk?

Mindful Listening to Your Body:

Follow-up Question: How attuned are you to the physical signals and cues your body provides?

Openness to Change:

Follow-up Question: How comfortable are you with adapting to change and embracing the unknown?

Trusting Your Intuition:

Follow-up Question: When faced with uncertainty, how often do you rely on your intuitive feelings to guide you?

Honoring Your Values:

Follow-up Question: In your decision-making, how closely do you align your choices with your core values?

TRUST AND INTUITION

Learning to trust myself is essential for nurturing intuitive thinking and discerning others. When I trust myself, I develop a deeper connection to my intuition, allowing me to recognize and interpret the subtle signals and insights that arise from within. By cultivating self-awareness and self-confidence, I become more attuned to my inner wisdom and gut feelings, enabling me to discern between authentic intuition and external influences or biases.

As I learn to trust myself, I also develop greater clarity and discernment in my interactions with others. By honing my intuitive abilities, I can sense the energy, intentions, and underlying motivations of those around me. This heightened awareness allows me to navigate social dynamics more effectively, identifying trustworthy individuals and recognizing red flags or warning signs.

Trusting myself empowers me to set boundaries, make decisions aligned with my values, and assert my needs and preferences confidently. By tuning into my intuition and trusting the guidance it provides, I cultivate a deeper sense of self-reliance and authenticity, enabling me to navigate life's complexities with clarity and confidence.

THE BLINDFOLDED TRUST WALK

CHALLENGE

Pair up with a friend or family member for a blindfolded trust walk. One person wears a blindfold while the other guides them through an obstacle course or around a designated area. The blindfolded person must trust their guide completely to navigate safely.

INSTRUCTIONS

Set up an Obstacle Course:

Create a simple obstacle course with objects like cushions, cones, or small obstacles.

Ensure a clear path for the blindfolded person to follow.

Choose Roles:

Decide who will be the blindfolded participant and who will be the guide.

Swap roles after completing the challenge.

Blindfolded Communication:

The guide cannot touch the blindfolded person but can only use verbal instructions to lead them.

Encourage clear and concise communication.

Start the Trust Walk:

The blindfolded person wears the blindfold and starts at the beginning of the course.

The guide stands at the starting point.

Navigate the Course:

The guide verbally directs the blindfolded person through the obstacle course.

The blindfolded person must trust their guide and follow the instructions.

Reflect and Swap Roles:

After completing the trust walk, reflect on the experience together.

Swap roles and repeat the challenge.

Follow-up Questions:

How did it feel to be blindfolded and trust someone else to guide you?

As the guide, how did you approach providing directions to ensure trust?

Were there moments of hesitation or doubt, and how did you overcome them?

How did effective communication play a role in the success of the challenge?

What did you learn about trust, collaboration, and communication from this experience?

TRUST TFOLLOW UP REFLECTION

Do I listen to my inner voice and honor my values, even in challenging situations?

_____

_____

Did I take 5 minutes to center myself with a quick meditation?

_____

_____

How am I continuing my self-care routine as I go through this course?

_____

_____

How can I listen to my inner voice and honor my values, even in challenging situations better?

_____

_____

TRUST-DAY 9

This experience left me in tears. Trust has always been a challenge for me; every time I let my guard down, I end up getting hurt. Over the years, I've learned to rely on myself because those who once promised love and protection turned out to be the ones who betrayed me the most. Recently, I've found more comfort, laughter, and connection with strangers than with friends and family I once leaned on.

This isn't about everyone, but enough to leave me with trust issues—a lingering wariness that never fully fades. Recently, I tried a version of the "trust game" with a friend, letting them take control of the day, from where we went to what we ate. I gave up control and allowed myself to be present, trusting their decisions.

But when we planned another outing, this person assumed they now had the final say in everything. My silence that first time seemed to signal that they were in charge, not that we were simply sharing an experience. It wasn't about collaboration; it became about control. Absolutely not.

Looking back, I'm glad I didn't do the traditional trust walk where you're led blindfolded. People recognize that as a game, a playful test of trust. But this? This was different. It revealed just how quickly some can overlook the balance of equal give and take.

It's going to be a long time before I let anyone blindfold me—literally or figuratively—again.

JOURNAL-DAY 10

Pick one exercise from the list to try today.

Journal Prompts

"Today, I am grateful for..."

List three things you are thankful for and reflect on why they bring you joy.

"In the next month, I want to accomplish..."

Set specific goals for the upcoming month and outline actionable steps.

"One thing I learned about myself today was..."

Reflect on a personal insight or realization from your day.

"The highlight of my day was..."

Describe the most positive or memorable moment from your day.

"What challenges did I face today, and how did I overcome them?"

Analyze obstacles and your strategies for overcoming them.

"If I could talk to my younger self, I would say..."

Offer advice or encouragement to your younger self.

"What are three things I love about myself?"

Focus on self-love and appreciation by listing positive qualities.

"Describe a place that brings me peace and why."

Create a vivid description of a calming place to evoke positive emotions.

"My favorite way to practice self-care is..."

Explore and write about activities that nurture your well-being.

"If today were a chapter in my life story, what would its title be?"

Summarize your day in a creative and symbolic way.

JOURNALING AND INTUITION

Journaling is a powerful tool for releasing creativity and nurturing intuitive thinking. By putting pen to paper, we engage in a process of self-expression and exploration that taps into our subconscious mind and unlocks hidden insights and ideas. Through free-writing, brainstorming, or exploring prompts, we can access our innermost thoughts, feelings, and desires, allowing our intuition to surface and guide us. Journaling also provides a safe space to experiment with new ideas, perspectives, and possibilities without fear of judgment or criticism. As we cultivate a regular journaling practice, we become more attuned to our intuition, learning to trust and follow its guidance in both creative endeavors and everyday decision-making. Whether it's through writing, drawing, or collage, journaling opens the door to endless opportunities for self-discovery, creativity, and intuitive growth.

CHARACTER SWAP JOURNALING

EXERCISE:

Choose a Character:

Pick a fictional character from a book, movie, or TV show.

Adopt Their Perspective:

Imagine you've swapped lives with this character for a day.

Journal as the Character:

Write about your day, experiences, and thoughts as if you were the chosen character.

Explore Their World:

Describe how the character would react to your daily activities, surroundings, and interactions.

Reflect on Contrasts:

Reflect on the differences between your usual perspective and the character's point of view.

Unleash Creativity:

Feel free to get creative! Write in the character's voice and bring their personality to life.

FOLLOW-UP QUESTIONS:

What surprised you most about experiencing life from this character's perspective?

Did adopting this character's mindset change how you approached your own challenges or joys?

How did this exercise impact your creativity and imagination?

What aspects of the character's personality did you find intriguing or challenging to embody?

Did you gain any new insights or empathy for the character through this exercise?

How might incorporating elements of this character's mindset enhance your own life?

JOURNAL FOLLOW UP REFLECTION

Do I listen to my inner voice and honor my values, even in challenging situations?

_____

_____

Did I take 5 minutes to center myself with a quick meditation?

_____

_____

How am I continuing my self-care routine as I go through this course?

_____

_____

How can I listen to my inner voice and honor my values, even in challenging situations better?

_____

_____

JOURNAL-DAY 10

One of the reasons I love journaling is because the moment I put pen to paper, I start manifesting what I'm writing. Whether it's expressing gratitude or making a simple grocery list, everything I want to change or acknowledge about myself always begins with a journal prompt. This time, journaling led me back to my personal "why," inspiring me to relaunch the blog on my website.

When I journal, I feel completely free. It's a space without judgment where I can unpack and process everything I'm thinking, feeling, wanting, or fearing. This honesty is essential; if I can't be truthful with myself about my emotions—my fears, failures, and hopes—how can I be genuine with others? And how can my tests become testimonies that might help heal others if I can't even acknowledge them privately?

I'm profoundly grateful to have found the peace and courage to share my journey in my own way.

SELF-DOUBT-DAY 11

Tips and Tricks for Overcoming Self-Doubt:

Positive Affirmations:

Tip: Create a list of positive affirmations tailored to counteract specific self-doubts.

Celebrate Achievements:

Tip: Keep a success journal to record and celebrate your achievements, big or small.

Set Realistic Goals:

Tip: Break down larger goals into smaller, achievable steps to build confidence.

Embrace Imperfection:

Tip: Understand that perfection is unattainable; embrace imperfections as part of the human experience.

Seek Support:

Tip: Share your self-doubts with a trusted friend, mentor, or therapist for support and perspective.

Visualize Success:

Tip: Create a mental image of yourself succeeding in various situations to boost confidence.

Follow-up Question: How does visualizing success impact your mindset and actions?

Celebrate Progress, Not Perfection:

Tip: Focus on progress rather than perfection, acknowledging steps forward.

Follow-up Question: What progress have you made recently that deserves recognition?

Self-Compassion:

Tip: Treat yourself with the same kindness and understanding you would offer a friend.

Follow-up Question: How can you cultivate a more compassionate and understanding relationship with yourself?

SELF-DOUBT AND INTUITION

Addressing and overcoming self-doubt is crucial for increasing and nurturing intuitive thinking. When we are plagued by self-doubt, our ability to trust and act upon our intuitive insights becomes compromised. Intuition often speaks in subtle, quiet whispers, and self-doubt can drown out these important signals, leading to hesitation and indecision.

To enhance intuitive thinking, it is essential to cultivate self-confidence and a positive self-image. This involves acknowledging and challenging negative self-talk, recognizing our strengths and accomplishments, and fostering a mindset that embraces the validity of our intuitive insights.

Practicing self-compassion is another key aspect of overcoming self-doubt. By treating ourselves with kindness and understanding, we create an environment that is conducive to intuitive thinking. Self-compassion allows us to acknowledge mistakes without dwelling on them, fostering resilience and a willingness to learn from our experiences.

Mindfulness practices can also be instrumental in overcoming self-doubt. Mindfulness helps us observe our thoughts without judgment, allowing us to detach from self-limiting beliefs and cultivate a more open and accepting mindset. This, in turn, creates space for intuitive insights to surface and be acknowledged.

As we work to diminish self-doubt, we not only strengthen our intuitive thinking but also open ourselves to a more authentic and empowered way of navigating life. Trusting our instincts becomes more natural, leading to better decision-making, improved self-awareness, and a deeper connection to our inner wisdom. In this way, addressing self-doubt becomes a powerful catalyst for nurturing and enhancing intuitive thinking.

SABOTAGING SELF-DOUBT

Here's a step-by-step exercise to combat self-doubt during intuitive training:

1. Set the Scene: Find a quiet and comfortable space where you can relax and focus without distractions. Take a few deep breaths to center yourself and clear your mind.

2. Identify the Doubts: Take a moment to acknowledge any self-doubt or negative thoughts that may be present. Write them down on a piece of paper or in a journal, giving them a voice and recognizing their existence.

3. Challenge the Doubts: For each doubt you've identified, challenge it by asking yourself: "Is this doubt based on fact or fear?" Explore whether there is any evidence to support the doubt or if it's simply a product of your inner critic.

4. Reframe the Doubts: Once you've identified the source of your doubts, reframe them into more positive and empowering statements. For example, if you doubt your intuitive abilities, reframe it as "I am capable of tapping into my intuition and trusting my inner guidance."

5. Practice Self-Compassion: Offer yourself kindness and compassion as you navigate through your doubts. Remind yourself that it's okay to feel uncertain or insecure at times, and that self-doubt is a natural part of the learning process.

6. Explore Different Pathways: Recognize that there are no wrong answers or failures in intuitive training, only different pathways

and experiences. Embrace the idea that each step you take, whether it leads to success or perceived failure, is an opportunity for growth and learning.

7. Experiment and Explore: Engage in intuitive exercises or activities that allow you to experiment and explore different approaches. Trust yourself to follow your intuition, even if it leads you down unexpected paths or yields unexpected results.

8. Reflect and Learn: After completing the exercise, take some time to reflect on your experience. What insights did you gain? What challenges did you encounter, and how did you overcome them? Use these reflections as opportunities for self-discovery and growth.

9. Celebrate Progress: Celebrate any progress you've made, no matter how small. Acknowledge your efforts and accomplishments, and recognize that each step forward is a testament to your resilience and determination.

10. Repeat Regularly: Make this exercise a regular part of your intuitive training routine. Consistent practice and self-reflection will help you build confidence, overcome self-doubt, and cultivate a deeper connection to your intuition over time.

SELF-DOUBT FOLLOW UP REFLECTION

Reflect on a recent decision or situation where I trusted myself. How did it feel, and what did I learn from the experience?

_____

_____

Consider moments when I felt doubt or hesitation. What were the factors that influenced my trust in those situations?

_____

_____

Are there patterns in my life where trusting myself consistently leads to positive outcomes?

_____

_____

How has the level of trust in myself evolved over time, and what contributed to this evolution?

_____

_____

SELF-DOUBT-DAY 11

I've come to realize that if I don't champion myself, no one else will. And even when I do, the people who should be supportive often aren't. Maybe it's jealousy, or maybe they're caught up in their own struggles, but I've learned that it's not my burden to carry.

Celebrating the small milestones along the way has become essential for me, especially when the ultimate goal feels so distant. If I don't take the time to acknowledge how far I've come, it's easy to lose sight of my progress, and that opens the door to doubt—wondering if I'll ever reach the "finish line."

This time, I'm recognizing that I've stayed committed to this journey, even if it hasn't unfolded exactly as I planned. There's space to forge my own path, and I'm discovering just that. The examples I've shared on trusting oneself intuitively are simply starting points, a framework.

Even for myself, I'm uncovering new, better, or more creative ways to tackle challenges. Instead of a traditional trust walk, I embarked on a trust trip, reflecting on how I trust myself to make the best choices for where I am right now. It's helped me combat any doubts that this project might become the "same old thing." It won't, because I'm constantly learning, experimenting with fresh approaches, and trusting that I have what it takes to succeed.

NATURE-DAY 12

NATURE HACKS

Daily Outdoor Ritual:

Tip: Establish a daily outdoor ritual, whether it's a morning walk or an evening nature sit.

Unplug in Nature:

Tip: Set aside dedicated time to unplug from technology and immerse yourself in nature.

Earthing or Grounding:

Tip: Practice earthing by walking barefoot on natural surfaces like grass or sand.

Follow-up Question: How did grounding yourself physically impact your sense of connection?

Outdoor Meditation:

Tip: Meditate outdoors, focusing on natural sounds, sensations, and the breath.

Follow-up Question: What insights or calmness did you gain from your outdoor meditation?

Nature Photography:

Tip: Capture the beauty of nature through photography, fostering a creative connection.

Follow-up Question:

How does photography enhance your appreciation for the natural world?

Sunrise or Sunset Ritual:

Tip: Experience the magic of sunrise or sunset regularly to connect with the changing colors of the sky.

NATURE AND INTUITION

Being in nature is profoundly important for nurturing and enhancing intuitive thinking. Nature has a way of grounding us, quieting the mind, and connecting us to our inner wisdom. When we immerse ourselves in natural environments, whether it's a forest, a mountain, or the ocean, we experience a sense of awe and wonder that transcends the ordinary.

One of the key ways nature enhances intuitive thinking is by promoting mindfulness and presence. In natural settings, we are more attuned to the present moment, free from the distractions and stressors of modern life.

Spending time in nature also provides opportunities for solitude and reflection, which are essential for deepening our intuitive awareness. In the quietude of natural spaces, we can engage in contemplative practices such as meditation, journaling, or simply sitting in stillness, allowing intuitive insights to emerge organically.

Overall, being in nature is an invaluable practice for nurturing and enhancing intuitive thinking. It offers a sanctuary for quiet reflection, a playground for sensory exploration, and a source of inspiration and wonder. By immersing ourselves in the beauty and majesty of the natural world, we cultivate a deeper connection to our intuition and tap into the boundless wisdom that resides within us.

THROUGH THE LENS OF NATURE

CHALLENGE:

Weekly Theme:

Choose a nature theme for the week (e.g., trees, water, flowers) to guide your photography.

Daily Snapshot:

Capture one photo each day that embodies the chosen theme.

Creative Angles:

Experiment with different angles, perspectives, and framing techniques to add creativity.

Macro Monday:

Dedicate Mondays to capturing close-up shots, focusing on the intricate details of nature.

Silhouette Storytelling:

Explore silhouette photography during sunrise or sunset, telling a visual story with shadows.

Texture Treasure Hunt:

Seek out and photograph various textures in nature, emphasizing the tactile elements.

Color Burst Wednesday:

Focus on vibrant colors in nature. Find and photograph the most eye-catching hues.

Weekend Wilderness:

Plan a weekend nature excursion, capturing the essence of a natural setting.

NATURE FOLLOW UP REFLECTION

How can I incorporate a daily outdoor ritual into my schedule?

_____

_____

Did I notice any patterns or recurring elements in my week of nature photography?

_____

_____

How can I continue incorporating nature photography into my routine beyond the challenge?

_____

_____

Create a digital or physical collage of my favorite photos from the challenge and share it with friends or on social media. How do I feel?

_____

_____

NATURE-DAY 12

I'm loving how much I'm trusting my intuition these days. My daily nature walks have become a sacred time to unplug from the world and truly connect with the Earth. I feel this deep urge to be in sync with nature, whether I'm walking barefoot in the backyard, swimming in my pool, or sitting by the fire pit. Each moment brings me a unique sense of peace and grounding with the elements.

The pool feels like a rebirth, a fresh start. Walking on the grass feels like a warm embrace from the Earth, while the fire stirs an energy within me—either an emerging desire or something that needs to be released. I've been paying close attention to how my emotions shift in different environments. I've always known I'm an outdoors girl—I love camping, hiking, and even simple moments of connection, like waving and smiling at strangers.

This all reminds me how much I love the unknown and how deeply the travel bug runs in me. There are so many beautiful wonders in the world, and I don't want to miss a single one. Staying put in my hometown would mean missing out on the joy, the happiness, and the natural beauty that's waiting out there. This week has powerfully reminded me to keep exploring—whether it's discovering hidden spots in my own neighborhood or venturing to new corners of the world. One thing's clear: I can't ground myself in nature from the couch.

DREAMS-DAY 13

Ever woke up with a feeling lingering from a dream? That gut reaction can be a clue, a nudge from our intuitive self. Dreams often untangle the messiness in our minds, bringing clarity through our subconscious thoughts.

Dreams tap into the depths of our emotions and show us what we might be overlooking in the hustle of our waking hours. So, next time you wake up with a vivid memory or a lingering emotion from a dream, write it down. It might just be your intuition leaving you a clue from the other side of your thoughts.

If you are having trouble remembering your dreams, here are some tips:

Create a Dream Journal:

Keep a notebook or use a dream journal app by your bedside. Jot down any fragments or feelings immediately upon waking. The act of recording your dreams signals to your brain that these experiences are important.

Set the Intention Before Bed:

Before falling asleep, tell yourself that you want to remember your dreams. This simple act can prime your mind to be more attentive to your dream experiences.

Wake Up Naturally:

If possible, allow yourself to wake up without an alarm. Abrupt awakenings can make it harder to recall dreams. If using an alarm, choose one with a gentle or gradual sound.

Stay Still Upon Waking:

When you wake up, try to remain still for a moment. Sometimes, the memories of dreams can fade quickly upon waking, and moving too abruptly can cause them to slip away.

Reflect Before Getting Up:

Take a moment to reflect on any images, feelings, or details from your dreams before getting out of bed. This brief pause can help solidify dream memories.

DREAMS AND INTUITION

Dreams play a vital role in tapping into deep subconscious emotions and are instrumental in nurturing and enhancing intuitive thinking and training. When we dream, our subconscious mind communicates with us through symbols, metaphors, and imagery, offering insights into our deepest fears, desires, and unresolved emotions.

One of the key ways dreams contribute to intuitive thinking is by providing a direct channel to our subconscious wisdom. Dreams bypass the filters of our conscious mind, allowing us to access intuitive insights and guidance that may be obscured during waking hours. By paying attention to recurring themes, symbols, and emotions in our dreams, we can uncover valuable information about our innermost thoughts and feelings, illuminating areas of our lives that may require attention or exploration.

Moreover, dreams offer a safe space for processing and integrating complex emotions and experiences. In dreams, we may encounter situations or scenarios that mirror real-life challenges or conflicts, providing an opportunity for catharsis and healing. By confronting and working through these emotions in the realm of dreams, we can gain clarity, resolution, and a deeper understanding of ourselves and our relationships.

Dreams also serve as a source of inspiration and creativity, fueling our imagination and expanding our intuitive capacities. Many artists, writers, and inventors throughout history have credited their dreams with providing them with breakthrough ideas and insights. By cultivating a practice of dream recall and interpretation, we can harness the creative potential of our subconscious mind, tapping into a wellspring of intuition and innovation.

In essence, dreams are a powerful tool for nurturing and enhancing intuitive thinking and training. They offer a window into the depths of our psyche, providing us with valuable insights, guidance, and inspiration. By paying attention to our dreams and honoring their messages, we can cultivate a deeper connection to our intuition, foster personal growth, and unlock the limitless potential of our subconscious mind.

FUTURE VISIONS: DREAMWEAVER CHALLENGE

CHALLENGE:

Future Focus:

Envision your ideal future scenario, whether it's personal, professional, or a blend of both.

Immersive Visualization:

Close your eyes and immerse yourself in the details of this future vision. Picture the surroundings, people, and the emotions you'd experience.

Intuitive Decision Path:

Allow your intuition to guide you in making decisions within your future daydream. Trust spontaneous insights that arise.

Sounds of Tomorrow:

Curate a playlist or ambient soundscape that embodies the energy and ambiance of your envisioned future.

Acting on Future Insights:

Throughout the day, follow through on intuitive hunches or decisions inspired by your daydreamed future.

Future Expressions:

Express your future vision creatively—whether through writing, drawing, or any artistic form—to solidify your aspirations.

Future Journal Entries:

Maintain a journal documenting any insights, ideas, or inspirations that emerge about your future during or after the daydream.

DREAMS FOLLOW UP REFLECTION

What aspects of your ideal future did you choose to focus on, and why?

_____

_____

Share a specific detail or moment from your daydreamed future that resonated strongly with you.

_____

_____

How did engaging your intuition in decision-making during the daydream influence your real-life choices?

_____

_____

Describe the sounds or music that accompanied your envisioned future. How did they enhance the atmosphere?

_____

_____

DREAMS -DAY 13

I'm so grateful to be in the process of remembering my dreams. Even if they don't come every night, when they do, I make sure to write them down—they always hold something profound for my conscious life. Since I started keeping a journal and pen by my bed, I've noticed I sleep so much better. Each morning, before anything else, I ask the universe what it wants me to remember from my dreams.

This is when the images come to me. For me, dreams are rarely about words; they're visual, filled with music and movement, almost like watching scenes unfold through the lens of a camera. It feels completely out-of-body, like I'm directing my life from a cosmic perspective. And maybe that's what dreaming is all about. When we dream, we step into other realms, glimpsing our lives as they could be, will be, or should have been. We all have free will, and sometimes people stray from the paths meant for them. I'm no exception.

Lately, my dreams have shifted from the past to visions of the future—images of what I want to manifest rather than what no longer exists. It's a clear sign that I'm moving forward, taking care of myself, and aligning with the best version of me for what lies ahead. I've learned to dream big and let go of the "how," trusting that if I can dream it, it's possible.

CREATIVITY -DAY 14

"Boost Your Intuition with Creativity: Quick Tips!"

Embrace Playfulness:

Tip: Approach creative activities with a sense of playfulness and curiosity.

Mindful Creation:

Tip: Practice mindfulness while engaging in creative activities, paying attention to the present moment.

Trusting Instincts in Writing:

Tip: In writing, trust your initial thoughts and write.

Visual Storytelling:

Tip: Use visual arts to tell a story, allowing intuition to guide the composition.

Example: Create a collage that represents your feelings/

Exploratory Music Creation:

Tip: Experiment with creating music without adhering to traditional structures.

Intuitive Movement:

Tip: Express yourself through spontaneous movement, letting your body guide the dance.

Found Object Art:

Tip: Create art using found objects, letting your intuition guide the selection and arrangement.

Collaborative Creations:

Tip: Collaborate with others in creative endeavors, allowing the merging of different intuitive perspectives.

Intuitive Cooking:

Tip: Approach cooking as a creative endeavor, trusting your instincts with flavors and ingredients.

Freeform Photography:

Tip: Capture moments spontaneously without adhering to traditional composition rules.

CREATIVITY AND INTUITION

One of the key ways creativity enhances intuitive thinking is by expanding our awareness and perspective. Creative pursuits such as art, music, writing, or problem-solving require us to think outside the box, challenging us to explore unconventional ideas and approaches. This openness to novelty and experimentation creates fertile ground for intuitive thinking to thrive, as we become more receptive to the subtle cues and signals that arise from within.

Creativity encourages us to trust in our intuition and follow our instincts, even when they lead us down unfamiliar paths. By embracing uncertainty and embracing the unknown, we tap into our innate ability to navigate complexity and ambiguity with confidence and resilience. This willingness to take risks and trust in our intuitive guidance is essential for fostering creativity and innovation.

Conversely, intuitive thinking enriches our creative endeavors by infusing them with authenticity, depth, and meaning. When we trust in our intuition, we connect more deeply with our innermost thoughts, emotions, and desires, allowing us to create from a place of genuine expression and passion. Intuitive insights often serve as catalysts for creative breakthroughs, inspiring us to explore new ideas, experiment with different techniques, and push the boundaries of our artistic vision.

In essence, creativity and intuitive thinking are integral components of a holistic approach to problem-solving, decision-making, and personal growth. By cultivating both creativity and intuition, we expand our capacity for innovation, deepen our connection to ourselves and others, and enrich our lives with meaning, purpose, and fulfillment. Whether through artistic expression, entrepreneurial endeavors, or everyday problem-solving, the synergy between creativity and intuitive thinking empowers us to embrace change, embrace uncertainty, and embrace the limitless possibilities of the human imagination.

SPARK YOUR INTUITION

CHALLENGE:

Pick Your Playground:

Choose a creative avenue from the tips provided (writing, painting, music, etc.).

Embrace Spontaneity:

Dive into your chosen activity without a predetermined plan. Let intuition guide your decisions.

Playful Timer:

Set a timer for a short burst of creative exploration (15-30 minutes).

Mix and Match:

Combine different creative elements or tips to infuse variety into your project.

Share the Joy:

If possible, share your creation or the process with a friend or fellow participant.

Reflect and Rejoice:

Take a moment to reflect on how intuition played a role in your creative journey. Celebrate the insights gained.

CREATIVITY FOLLOW UP REFLECTION

What feelings and insights emerged during the creative process?

_____

_____

What patterns or recurring themes did I notice in my creative work influenced by intuition?

_____

_____

How can these intuitive practices be applied in other areas of my life?

_____

_____

Final Thoughts?

_____

_____

CREATIVITY -DAY 14

I love painting—not for money, but for peace. There's a unique joy in getting lost with a glass of wine, some jazz, and a blank canvas. Painting evil eyes in various forms has become a favorite ritual of mine; to me, they're powerful symbols of protection. And honestly, I welcome all the protection I can get—whether it's self-created, divinely given, or from others watching over me. Each evil eye I paint reminds me that the eyes are windows to the soul.

When people visit my home, I notice how they respond to my artwork, especially the evil eyes. If someone feels uneasy around them, I observe quietly. Their reactions tell me a lot. If my creativity makes someone uncomfortable, it's a sign that we may not be spiritually aligned, and I become mindful about letting that kind of energy into my space.

So, I'll keep painting—whether the sun is shining or the rain is pouring. Seeking clarity and peace has no downside. What began as a personal outlet soon became something I shared with others. People started asking me to paint and even pray over pieces for them. What was once a private passion has now grown into something that brings me both peace and a source of income. I've learned that even a simple hobby can hold value—monetary and otherwise—because I honor my own creativity.

This is the last of my personal reflections. Over time, I've come to understand the importance of keeping a part of my journey sacred, just for myself.

Moving forward (Days 15-30,) I'll be sharing stories from an anonymous client I worked with this year, and how I helped them diversify their purpose, finding both fulfillment and financial freedom along the way.

CREATIVITY FOLLOW UP REFLECTION

What specific techniques or practices did you learn during the intuition training course?

_____

_____

How do you feel your intuition has developed or changed as a result of taking the course?

_____

_____

Were there any particular exercises or activities in the course that stood out to you as especially helpful or impactful?

_____

_____

Did the course provide any practical strategies for incorporating intuition into your daily life or decision-making process?

_____

_____

INTUITION TRAINING

I AM

The I AM deck was created as a way of teaching me how to affirm myself. How often have I looked outside my own affirmation to receive outside validation AND let that dictate my self-esteem, self-worth and self- love?

Does that even make sense to look outside of ourselves to define ourselves. *I made this deck because I wanted to remember*

I WANT

That's a good hard look in the mirror which is why I also created the I WANT deck because there were a lot of things that I needed to work on as well.

We are forgetting how to feel and we are forgetting that feelings are a strength not a weakness. Sharing your feelings are a strength not a weakness. Sharing your feelings is the most strong

that I have the ability to independently investigate the truth from myself. In order to trust and discern what I've felt being my thoughts and feelings or someone else's was I had to create, and define who I was independently of anyone else in my life, anything that I do or where I came from.

and vulnerable thing a person can do. And to do it fearlessly, and honestly with as much dignity and grace as you can is, the goal. These cards are a reminder that we are human beings, not human branding's, and if we worried a little less about our brand and more about our being, both might expand beyond our wildest dreams.

HOW TO USE YOUR INTUITION

Page 105

CREATED BY MAYA LYNNE ROBINSON

DIRECTIONS

Pick A Card, As Needed To Increase Your Intuitive Mindset, Emotional Intelligence And Overall Well-being.

ONE CARD SPREAD

DATE

CARD

1. WHAT SHOULD I FOCUS ON?

TWO CARD SPREAD

| 1 | 2 |

RETAIN	RELEASE
FEELINGS	THOUGHTS
NEED	WANT
PROBLEM	SOLUTION

THREE CARD SPREAD

| 1 | 2 | 3 |

PAST	PRESENT	FUTURE
OPTION 1	OPTION 2	ADVICE
EMBRACE	ACCEPT	LET GO
HEAD	HEART	SPIRIT

FIVE CARD SPREAD

| 1 | 2 | 3 |

| 4 | 5 |

1. WHAT I WANT
2. ENERGY NEEDED
3. CURRENT ENERGY
4. HOW TO GET ALIGNED
5. LETTING GO OF THE HOW

NINE CARD SPREAD

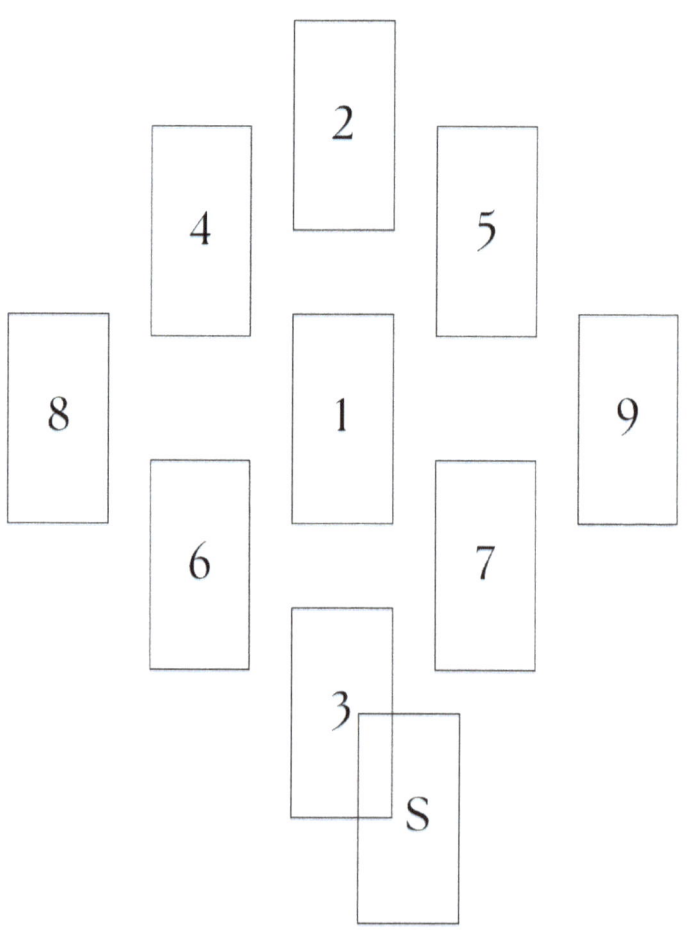

1. WHERE AM I NOW?
2. WHAT AM I DOING WELL?
3. MY PAST/ WHAT I GAINED?
4. MY CAREER AND FINANCES
5. WHAT AM I THINKING ABOUT?
6. MY FUTURE/ WHERE CAN I GO?
7. WHAT AM I PASSIONATE ABOUT?
8. S-SHADOW DECK TRIGGER- W/ #3
9. WHAT CHALLENGES AM I FACING?
10. MY EMOTIONS AND RELATIONSHIPS

MODULE 4
PURPOSE

HELLO

This planner was designed to assist you in a number of ways.

Find your purpose. When you make the time to ask yourself the tough questions and take the time to figure out the answers, your life fills with meaning.

Organize your goals. Hold yourself accountable for achieving your goals by giving yourself milestones along the way.

Create healthy choices. Assist you in creating healthy mental and physical habits.

Affirm your growth. As you hold yourself accountable, you begin to see the finish-line and it's motivating!

Allow this planner to guide you to a more self-improved YOU.

And remember, you are allowed to grow, which includes changing your mind about who you are and what you want. The answer, your purpose, will never be wrong if it brings you fulfillment. Shine (on purpose.)

Enjoy!

BE THE CHANGE I WANT TO SEE

LIFE PATH NUMBERS AND PURPOSE

Your life path number provides valuable insights into your personality, strengths, and potential challenges, which can help guide you towards discovering your purpose.

Understanding Your Natural Abilities: Each life path number is associated with specific traits and characteristics. By understanding these traits, you can identify your natural talents and abilities. For example, if you have a life path number 3, which is associated with creativity and self-expression, you may find your purpose in artistic pursuits or communication-related fields.

Recognizing Your Passions: Your life path number can also highlight the areas of life that resonate most deeply with you. For instance, if you have a life path number 5, associated with adventure and freedom, you may feel most fulfilled when exploring new experiences or advocating for social change. Recognizing your passions can guide you towards career paths or hobbies that align with your purpose.

Navigating Challenges: Your life path number can also shed light on potential challenges or obstacles you may encounter along your journey. Understanding these challenges allows you to proactively address them and develop resilience. For example, if you have a life path number 8, associated with success and abundance, you may need to overcome issues related to power dynamics or materialism to fully embody your purpose.

Embracing Personal Growth: Ultimately, your life path number serves as a roadmap for personal growth and self-discovery. As you navigate life's ups and downs, your understanding of your life path can deepen, leading to greater clarity and alignment with your purpose. By embracing opportunities for learning and development, you can continue to evolve and live a purpose-driven life.

In summary, your life path number serves as a valuable tool for self-reflection and exploration, helping you uncover your unique purpose and live a fulfilling and meaningful life.

CALCULATING YOUR LIFE PATH NUMBER

Calculating your life path number is easy! Follow these steps:

Write down your birthdate in numeric format. For example, if you were born on July 15, 1990, your birthdate would be written as 07/15/1990.

Add up all the digits in your birthdate separately. For example:

Month: 0 + 7 = 7   Day: 1 + 5 = 6

Year: 1 + 9 + 9 + 0 = 19

If the year total has multiple digits, add those digits together until you get a single-digit number. In this example, 1 + 9 = 10, and then 1 + 0 = 1.

Add the month, day, and year totals together. Using the example:

Month: 7   Day: 6

Year: 1 Total: 7 + 6 + 1 = 14

If the total has multiple digits, repeat step 3 until you get a single-digit number. In this example, 1 + 4 = 5.

Your life path number is the final single-digit number you calculated. In this example, the life path number is 5.

That's it! You've calculated your life path number. Now you can explore what it means for your life's journey.

How quickly you complete your purpose plan in the next seven days is up to you. For some sections, you may start and then go back and finish up later. Some sections you haven't thought much about, if any, and others will be easy to complete. Trust yourself.

THE NORTH NODE IS THE GOAL

Your life path is like your personal roadmap to your purpose! Each life path number reflects a different journey, guiding you towards fulfilling your unique destiny.

Life Path 1: You're a natural leader, here to blaze your own trail and inspire others with your independence and ambition.

Life Path 2: You thrive in partnerships and love bringing harmony to your relationships. Your purpose lies in cooperation and teamwork.

Life Path 3: Creativity is your superpower! You're here to express yourself and spread joy through your art, words, or ideas.

Life Path 4: You're the rock-solid foundation, here to build stability and security for yourself and others through hard work and practicality.

Life Path 5: Adventure awaits! You're here to embrace change, explore new horizons, and inspire others to break free from limitations.

Life Path 6: Your purpose is all about love and nurturing. You're here to bring balance and harmony to your family, community, or the world.

Life Path 7: You're a seeker of truth and wisdom, here to uncover the deeper meaning of life and share your insights with others.

Life Path 8: You're destined for success and abundance! Your purpose is to achieve financial and material mastery while making a positive impact on the world.

Life Path 9: Compassion is your calling card. You're here to serve humanity and make the world a better place through your empathy and humanitarian efforts.

No matter your life path number, remember that you're exactly where you're meant to be on your journey to fulfilling your purpose!

CALCULATING YOUR NORTH NODE

To calculate your North Node in astrology, you need your exact date, time, and place of birth. Once you have this information, follow these steps:

1. Create your natal chart: Use an astrology website or software to generate your natal chart based on your birth details. This chart will show the positions of the planets, signs, and houses at the time of your birth.

2. Locate your North Node: Look for the symbol " " in your natal chart. This symbol represents the North Node. It will be located in one of the twelve astrological signs and one of the twelve houses.

3. Determine the sign: Note the sign in which your North Node is located. Each sign represents different qualities and lessons that you are meant to embrace and develop in this lifetime.

4. Determine the house: Note the house in which your North Node is located. Each house represents different areas of life where you are meant to focus your growth and development.

Once you have identified your North Node sign and house, you can research and explore the qualities, themes, and lessons associated with them to gain insight into your soul's purpose and direction in this lifetime. Keep in mind that the North Node is often considered the point of destiny or spiritual growth, guiding you towards fulfilling your highest potential and evolving into your true self.

LIFE PATH + NORTH NODE = PURPOSE

The concept of "Life Path + North Node = Purpose" is rooted in astrology and spiritual philosophy, suggesting that by aligning our life path with the qualities and lessons associated with our North Node, we can uncover our true purpose and fulfillment in life.

In astrology, the North Node represents the point in our birth chart that indicates the direction in which we are meant to grow and evolve in this lifetime. It symbolizes our soul's journey and the lessons we are here to learn. The South Node, its counterpart, represents our past experiences and tendencies that we may need to release or transcend in order to fully embrace our North Node path.

The Life Path, on the other hand, refers to the journey we take in life, encompassing our experiences, challenges, and opportunities for growth. It reflects the choices we make and the paths we follow as we navigate through the various stages and transitions of life.

When we combine the Life Path with the North Node, we are essentially aligning our personal journey with our soul's purpose. By consciously working to embody the qualities and themes associated with our North Node sign and house placement, we can tap into our innate talents, strengths, and potential for growth.

For example, if someone's North Node is in the sign of Aries and the first house, they may be meant to embrace qualities such as courage, independence, and self-assertion in order to fulfill their life purpose. By stepping out of their comfort zone, taking initiative, and pursuing their passions with confidence, they can align their actions with their soul's calling and experience a greater sense of fulfillment and purpose in life.

Ultimately, the concept of "Life Path + North Node = Purpose" encourages us to explore the deeper dimensions of our astrological chart and spiritual journey, guiding us towards a path of self-discovery, personal growth, and alignment with our soul's true calling. Through self-awareness, conscious intention, and alignment with our North Node path, we can unlock our potential and live a life that is rich in meaning, purpose, and fulfillment.

PURPOSE PLANNER

Unlock your potential and live with intentionality with the Purpose Planner! Designed to help you track your goals, stay organized, and align your daily actions with your purpose, this planner is your roadmap to a more fulfilling life. With dedicated sections for goal setting, reflection, and action planning, the Purpose Planner empowers you to prioritize what truly matters and take meaningful steps towards your dreams. Print the pages or use GoodNotes or the equivalent for your digital needs.

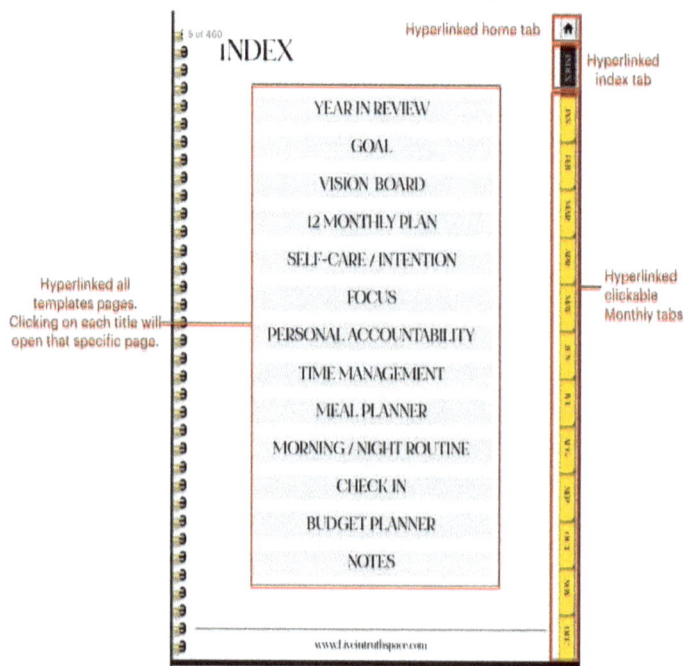

THE NIGHT BEFORE

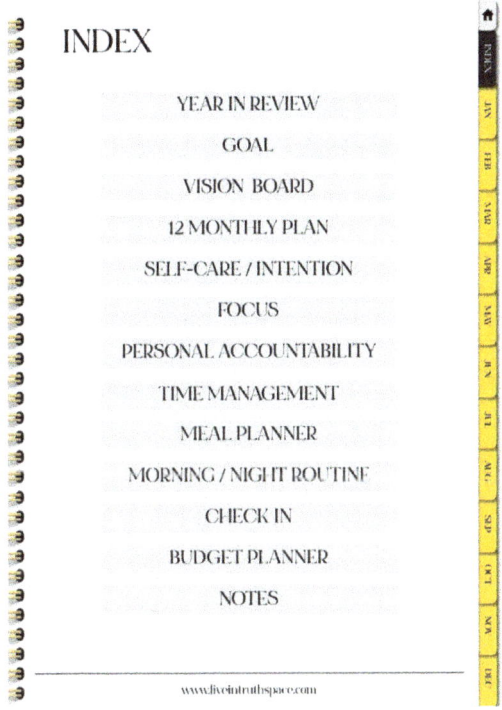

The night before you begin, take some time to fill out these sections as best as you can. Set a timer for an hour and dive in! You'll quickly see how much (or how little) of your life you've really planned out. That's why this process is so important! Having a sense of purpose—a goal to focus on—helps us navigate through life with meaning. It's not about how much money you have; it's about finding your true calling, your destiny.

Your calling is not linked to a profession, but a profession can help you showcase your calling.

INDEX-DAY 15

After working hard on my intuition, I do this next part differently every time. Sometimes, I am aware of the things I need to work on in my purpose plan, so the things I'm doing well. I can fly through those sections because things haven't changed.

This is also the section I check once a month to ensure I'm on track or if I've changed my mind about certain aspects of my journey. I read the entire INDEX I created for myself at the beginning of the journey.

If you are reading this for the first time, you will spend the majority of your week here. Once you know where you are and where you want to go, setting shorter-term goals will be much easier. When I first started doing this section, I spent three days on it.

EACH GOAL HAS THREE SUBCATEGORIES

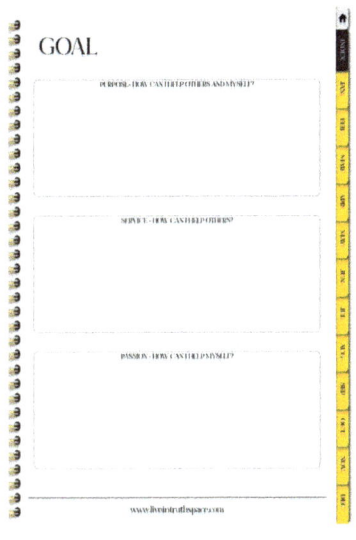

1. *That helps you - shine and uplift*

2. *That heals you - heART heals*

3. *That scares you - not in comfort zone*

VISION BOARD

Now, put it all together. Write your three goals here. Remember, you can change your mind as your purpose plan becomes more defined.

Discover Your Calling

GOALS AND VISIONS-DAY 16

When I know what I want, this page is easy to fill out, but if I'm unsure, it takes a while. I keep a pen and paper near me on this day so that anything that sparks joy or interest comes to my mind, I write it down. It, more often than not, contains clues about what GOALS I should be moving toward in my life.

What I love about these sections is I typically don't write; I use images/visuals to show me the VISION. I strongly believe in the phrase, If you can see it, you can achieve it. Manifestation is merely the creation of what I envision for myself. These goals can be scary because they come with great responsibility, and I desire to master discernment, who and what will take me off my path and what won't. There is no wrong way to see the future, whether words or images. I love to let my imagination and creativity run free.

EVERYTHING IS CONNECTED

YEAR IN REVIEW

January	MY BIGGEST ACCOMPLISHMENTS
February	
March	SOMETHING NEW I TRIED
April	
May	SOMETHING NEW I TRIED
June	
July	THINGS I WANT TO CHANGE/LEARN OR TIPS IN THE NEXT YEAR
August	
September	
October	
November	
December	

www.liveintruthspace.com

YEAR IN REVIEW

January	MY BIGGEST ACCOMPLISHMENTS
February	
March	SOMETHING NEW I TRIED
April	
May	SOMETHING NEW I TRIED
June	
July	THINGS I WANT TO CHANGE/LEARN OR TIPS IN THE NEXT YEAR
August	
September	
October	
November	
December	

www.liveintruthspace.com

PAST
Focus on what you achieved and what challenged you.challenged you.

PRESENT
Focus on what you are and what challenges you.

FUTURE
Focus on what you want and what challenged you.

Discover Your Calling

REVIEW-DAY 17

Doing this planner every year has allowed me to see when I am living my best life or when I feel depressed by life. I see what events in the world and my life caused me to elevate or decline spiritually when working towards fulfilling my highest potential- my purpose.

When I look at the past, present, and future all on one page, I remember how small I truly am in the grand scheme of the world. If, when I pass away, everything that can be said about me can be done in 500 words or less in an obituary, then I can look at two years of my life on this page.

This page reminds me to be a doer, not just a dreamer. Plans without action are just wishes, and this page keeps me mindful of my life plans. It's a reminder that everything I want is possible if I plan, pray, and act from a place of gratitude and humility.

I ask myself what I learned from last year's highlights and how I want to incorporate what I did into my future. This page is a lie detector test. When I do the intuitive work, and then I work on this page, anything that doesn't ring authentic to me will create pain in my body. Because I am tapped in, I tip myself off to what doesn't serve my more extraordinary being or that of the world.

I am not perfect, but I am honest. That's why it's called a REVIEW. Once again, I am comparing what I've done with what I want to do.

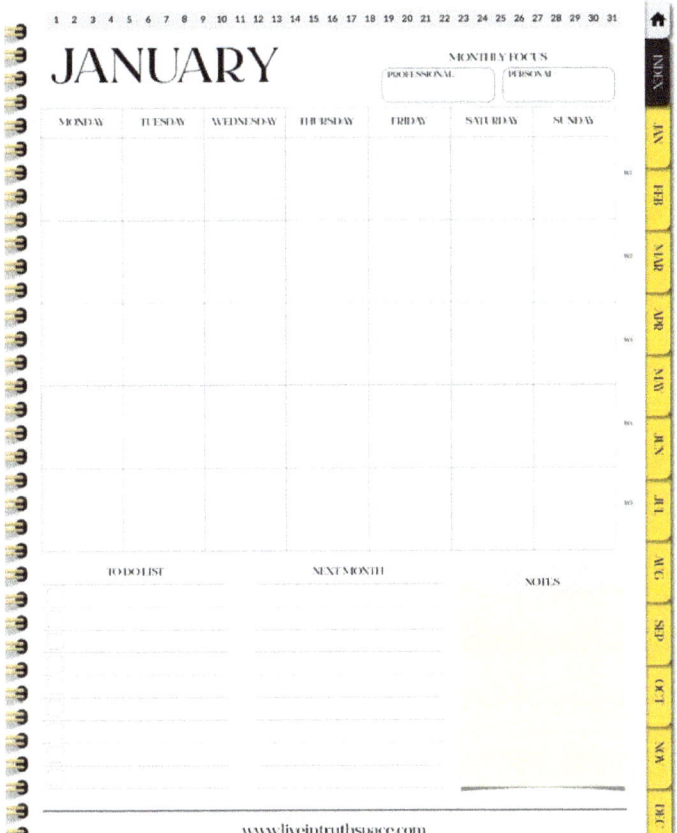

Start with the current month. This planner is customizable so you can start anytime.

1. Start with the major personal and professional goals for the month.

2. Add any essential events/dates toward your goals on the monthly page.

3. Any tasks, thoughts, or next month's thoughts should be added.

Feel free to write all through the workbook.

MONTHLY-DAY 18

Once I look at my Year in Review section, I realize what I did and did not do the year before, which either elevated or stunted my potential. It had a lot to do with my Time Management and Personal Accountability. I had to break this down into quarters. I looked at the overall goals that I wanted for the year. I created six big goals broken down into 18 milestones along the way.

Here's a sample of three goals I had in 2023, broken down into nine milestones, for reference.

GOALS - PERSONAL

TRAVEL

TRAVEL

US CITY I HAVE NEVER VISITED

EUROPE

ASIA

GROWTH

FORGIVENESS

INTUITIVE MASTERY

POSITIVE SELF-TALK

SELF-CARE

EXERCISE

FUN

HEALTHY EATING

I did everything on my list that year. This year, I am getting more specific about my goals, such as why I want to go to a US city I've never visited and which foreign city I want to visit and what do I want to learn. But most importantly, I'm making choices about my life and how I want to live it.

WEEKLY PLAN

WEEK OF:

MONDAY

TUESDAY

WEDNESDAY

THURSDAY

FRIDAY

SATURDAY

SUNDAY

GOALS

TO DO LIST

www.liveintruthspace.com

Here, you will take every week and break it down into seven days of progress. Write any goals for the week towards your monthly goals here.

Discover Your Calling

WEEKLY-DAY 9

Once I had broken everything down into a MONTHLY schedule, I made the WEEKLY. The thing about the weekly is I only focus on the current and upcoming weeks. I have learned that if I do more than this, there is the ability to over-plan my life and leave very little room for spontaneity and freedom,

I look at my goals for the year and the next, and I break them down by week. Then, I focus on the first two weeks. This is also where I put my to-do list and any notes I may have because flipping through a digital planner can be daunting, but if you have everything conveniently closer, the ability to use the planner becomes greater than if they were on separate pages.

I place any quotes, affirmations, appointments, and ideas on this page. What I love about the weekly pages is their ability to read like a journal. When I look at my planner and see all the things I've been doing for that week, it often jogs back into my memory of how I was feeling during this time, as well. The words I use, the tasks that get completed, and the ones that get pushed aside tell me what my strengths and challenges are.

I look at the weekly daily, and if a day is particularly hectic, I pull out the DAILY pages. When I have those super busy days, I have to write it all out to see my day and most efficiently tackle the tasks I had laid out for myself.

Finally, if any days are particularly heavy, you should use a daily planner. Each day has its daily in the purpose planner

Check on you, friend!

Remember to check on you once a week and see how you're feeling. This is a safe space. You don't have to share this with anyone if you don't want to.

DAILY-DAY 20

I love DAILY pages because all of my OCD comes tumbling out. I have days when there is so much going on that I can't think. The night before a big day like this, the last thing I do is create a DAILY page. It's also the first thing I look at in the morning when making tea or coffee.

When I know I have created a structure around a hectic day, a sense of peace surrounds me. This page gives me the structure I need to be completely task-oriented.

I also added an area for Gratitude here as a reminder that through the day's craziness, there is still a lot for me to be thankful for.

CHECK IN

What happened?
_____
_____

What am i feeling?
_____
_____

What are some solutions? What gives me faith?
_____
_____

How am i growing from this?
_____
_____

Check on YOU, friend!
_____
_____

Remember to check on you once a week and see how you're feeling. This is a safe space. You don't have to share this with anyone if you don't want to.

CHECK IN-DAY 15

I have been guilty of doing all the steps but not checking in on how the process is making me feel or teaching me emotionally. This method requires the same amount of emotional intelligence for the amount of rewiring of my mental intelligence that it forces me to use.

My thoughts and feelings matter, too. I have worked hard to teach myself that it's okay not to overshare how you're feeling with others. What matters is checking on myself and how what I am doing for myself is making me feel.

Check-ins are healthy and easy for me because I'm the type of person who talks out loud to themselves, even when others are around. I have learned to live in the 3D and 5D worlds simultaneously and observe my behavior and energy when working through trauma and curses.

This is the most innovative step I could have added. It was one that I didn't initially have because I do this naturally, but after facilitating this course with many people, the feedback I received was, please help remind me that it's okay to check on me and put myself first. Check-ins are designed so that you keep sight of your goals and focus and keep sight of yourself.

Check-ins are a beautiful way of honoring yourself—your needs, wants, feelings, and insecurities—in a safe environment. They are meant for your eyes only.

CHECK IN

What happened?

What am i feeling?

What are my feats and insecurities surrounding the situation?

What are my feats and insecurities surrounding the situation?

How am i growing from this?

BUDGET PLANNING AND PURPOSE

Budget planning with a purpose is essential for achieving financial success and realizing our goals and aspirations. Here's how budget planning and having a clear purpose correlate:

1. Alignment of Spending: When we budget with a purpose, we allocate our financial resources towards our goals and priorities. This alignment ensures that our spending reflects what truly matters to us, whether it's saving for a home, paying off debt, traveling, or investing in our education or career advancement.

2. Motivation and Focus: Having a purpose gives us motivation and focus when budgeting. Knowing why we are budgeting and what we are working towards helps us stay disciplined and committed to our financial plan, even when faced with temptations or setbacks.

3. Decision Making: Budget planning with a purpose guides our decision-making process. It helps us distinguish between needs and wants, prioritize our spending, and make informed choices that align with our long-term goals and values.

4. Measurable Goals: A purpose-driven budget includes specific, measurable financial goals that we strive to achieve. These goals serve as benchmarks for tracking our progress and celebrating our successes along the way, keeping us motivated and accountable.

5. Financial Security and Freedom: Budgeting with a purpose lays the foundation for financial security and freedom. By managing our money wisely and directing it towards our goals, we build a solid financial future and create opportunities for ourselves and our loved

ones.

6. Peace of Mind: Knowing that our financial decisions are guided by a clear purpose brings peace of mind. It reduces stress and anxiety about money, knowing that we are taking proactive steps to achieve our dreams and aspirations.

In essence, budget planning with a purpose empowers us to take control of our finances, live with intentionality, and create a life that aligns with our values and priorities. It allows us to turn our dreams into actionable plans and take steps towards realizing them, one budget at a time.

CHECK IN

Description	Income Source	Amount

Monthly	
Total Income	
Total Budget	
Total Savings	
Total Expenses	
Total Income	

Notes

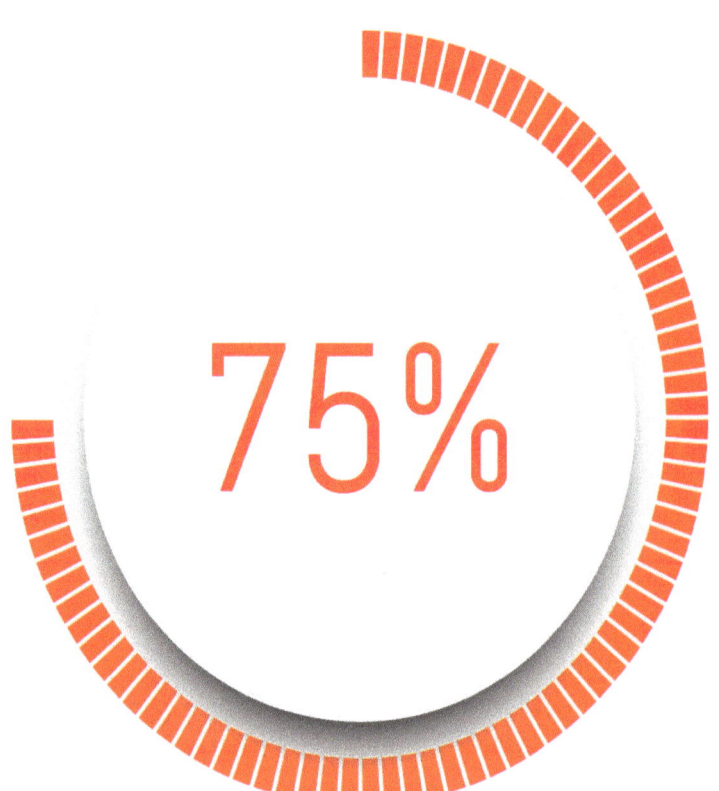

MODULE 5
DIVERSIFY YOUR BUSINESS

DIVERSIFY YOUR PURPOSE

Diversifying my purpose by incorporating passion, purpose, and service opportunities is immensely important. When I solely focus on a single aspect of my life, it limits my growth and hinders my ability to make a meaningful impact. Passion fuels my motivation and joy, driving me to explore and pursue activities that bring fulfillment. Purpose directs my actions with my core values and long-term goals. Service opportunities allow me to extend myself beyond personal gain and contribute to the well-being of others and society as a whole.

Multiple income streams, or diversifying purpose as I call them, have become the only means of survival in a money-hungry economy.

PURPOSE

HOW CAN I HELP MYSELF AND OTHERS?

SERVICE

HOW CAN I HELP OTHERS?

I AM

HOW CAN I HELP MYSELF?

DIVERSIFY YOUR PURPOSE

Executive Summary

Goals

Mission & Vision

Service Offering

Meet The Team

Marketing Plan

SWOT Analysis

Check Lists

Notes and Thoughts

_____

_____

_____

CLIENT: SARAH (PURSUING PASSION IN LOS ANGELES)

Case Study: Pursuing Passion in Los Angeles

Client Profile:

Name: Sarah Thompson

Age: 34

Location: Los Angeles, California

Marital Status: Unmarried

Family: No children

Background:

Sarah Thompson has been working as a corporate event planner for the past eight years in Los Angeles. While she excels in her role, managing large-scale events for prestigious clients, she finds herself increasingly disenchanted with her career. Despite the financial stability and professional success, Sarah feels unfulfilled and lacks a sense of purpose in her current 9 to 5 profession.

Challenges:

Lack of Fulfillment: Sarah struggles with a lack of personal fulfillment in her corporate role. While she enjoys the challenges and dynamics of event planning, she feels disconnected from her work's deeper meaning.

Creative Urge: Sarah has always been drawn to creativity and self-expression. She harbors a passion for photography and has recently started exploring painting as a means of artistic expression.

Fear of Change: Despite her dissatisfaction with her current career, Sarah is hesitant to make a drastic change. The stability and financial security provided by her corporate job serve as significant barriers to pursuing her creative passions full-time.

Uncertainty: Sarah is uncertain about how to transition from her current profession to a more creative pursuit. She lacks clarity on potential career paths, income stability, and the practical steps needed to make her passion a viable profession.

Goals:

Find Fulfillment: Sarah's primary goal is to find a career path that aligns with her passions and provides a sense of purpose and fulfillment.

Explore Creativity: Sarah wants to explore her creative talents further and potentially turn her passion for photography and painting into a fulfilling career.

Achieve Balance: Sarah aims to strike a balance between pursuing her creative passions and maintaining financial stability.

Overcome Fear: Sarah seeks to overcome her fear of change and take actionable steps towards transitioning into a more fulfilling career path.

Proposed Action Plan:

Self-Reflection: Sarah will engage in deep self-reflection to identify her core values, interests, and long-term aspirations. This process will help her gain clarity on what truly matters to her and guide her career decisions.

·Skills Assessment: Sarah will assess her skills and strengths, both *in her current profession and in her creative pursuits. Identifying transferable skills will enable her to leverage her corporate experience while transitioning into a new field.*

Networking and Mentorship: Sarah will actively seek out mentors and network with professionals in the creative industry. Building connections with individuals who have successfully transitioned from corporate careers to creative professions will provide her with valuable insights and guidance.

Education and Training: Sarah will invest in further education and training to enhance her skills in photography and painting. Enrolling in workshops, courses, or joining artistic communities will help her refine her craft and build credibility in her chosen creative field.

Side Hustle: Sarah will explore opportunities to pursue her creative passions as a side hustle initially. This will allow her to test the waters, gain experience, and generate additional income while still working in her corporate job.

Financial Planning: Sarah will develop a comprehensive financial plan to ensure a smooth transition from her corporate career to a creative profession. This plan will include budgeting, saving, and exploring potential sources of funding or grants for artists.

Mindset Shift: Sarah will work on shifting her mindset from fear and uncertainty to one of possibility and resilience. Adopting a growth mindset will empower her to embrace challenges, learn from failures, and pursue her dreams with confidence.

Conclusion:

Sarah Thompson's journey towards finding fulfillment and purpose in her career involves a strategic blend of self-reflection, skill development, networking, and financial planning. By embracing her creative passions and taking proactive steps towards transitioning into a more fulfilling profession, Sarah can embark on a rewarding and meaningful career path tailored to her interests and aspirations.

IF YOU ARE EXPERIENCING ANY OF THIS BACKSTORY, THIS COURSE IS A GREAT FIT FOR YOU.

EXECUTIVE SUMMARY

Think of the executive summary as the front door to your business plan, a snapshot inviting anyone to understand your business quickly. This is where we distill the essence of your business—its mission, vision, and key highlights—into a concise yet compelling overview. Working together, we'll weave the unique story of your business, highlighting its strengths, goals, and the value it brings to the market. The executive summary serves as a guide, setting the tone for the entire business plan and making a powerful first impression on potential investors, partners, or stakeholders. Let's collaborate closely to ensure it reflects your venture's true spirit and potential.

To write one, keep it simple and friendly:

1. Introduction: Start by introducing your business and what it does in a nutshell. Imagine you're telling a friend who knows nothing about your business – what would you say to get them excited?

2. Highlight the Key Points: Summarize the most important parts of your business plan, like your unique selling point, target market, and financial projections. Think of it as the highlight reel – what are the juiciest bits you want people to know?

3. Keep It Brief: Aim for around one to two pages max. You want to give enough information to pique interest but not overwhelm the reader with too much detail.

4. Be Clear and Concise: Use simple language and avoid jargon or technical terms that might confuse people. Remember,

you're trying to make a quick and easy-to-understand impression.

5. End Strong: Finish with a bang! Reiterate why your business is awesome and why people should care. Leave them wanting more!

By following these steps, you'll create an executive summary that grabs attention, highlights the best parts of your business, and leaves a lasting impression on anyone who reads it. Happy summarizing!

GOAL

Consider the goals section of your business plan as the roadmap that charts the course for your venture. It's not just a list of aspirations; it's a strategic plan that we create together to guide your business toward success. By clearly defining short-term and long-term objectives, we establish measurable targets  *that help track progress and stay focused. These goals become the benchmarks against which we measure success, helping you steer the ship with purpose. Through our collaborative efforts, we'll articulate not just what you want to achieve but also how we plan to get there, ensuring that every step aligns with the broader vision for your business.*

Sarah has three goals that I see immediately: open a creative studio, painting/photography classes, and event planning.

Goal 1

_____

Goal 2

_____

Goal 3

_____

MISSION STATEMENT

Think of a mission statement like the heart and soul of your business – it's what keeps you focused and guides everything you do. It's super important because it tells the world why your business exists and what it's all about. Plus, it helps you and your team stay on track and motivated.

To write one, keep it simple and friendly:

Define Your Purpose: Start by thinking about why your business exists. What problem are you solving or what value are you providing to people? Imagine you're telling a friend why you're starting this business – what would you say?

Be Clear and Concise: Your mission statement should be short and sweet, like a catchy slogan. Aim for just one or two sentences that capture the essence of your business.

Focus on Values: Think about what's important to you and your business. Is it innovation, customer satisfaction, sustainability, or something else? Your mission statement should reflect these values.

Inspire Others: Your mission statement should not only resonate with you but also inspire others, like customers, employees, and investors. It should make them excited to be a part of what you're doing.

Review and Refine: Once you've written your mission statement, review it regularly to make sure it still aligns with your business goals and values. It's okay to tweak it as your business evolves.

By following these steps, you'll create a mission statement that captures the essence of your business, inspires others, and keeps you focused on your goals. It's like your North Star – guiding you on your journey to success!

PASSION

Sarah has a passion for painting and photography.

Identify how you can help yourself.

PASSION

Identify how you can help yourself.

PASSION

Identify how you can help yourself.

Sarah has a purpose in connecting and being a connector through creative means. This desire is the reason for her pursuit of a creative studio space.

PASSION

Identify how you can help others and yourself.

SERVICE

Sarah has strong skills in event planning, which will allow her to make money and connect with people after hours.

Identify how you can help others.

SERVICE

Identify how you can help others.

MEET THE TEAM

Name the players and their positions.

SARAH
OWNER & CREATIVE DIRECTOR

TBA
INSTRUCTORS

TBA
ADMIN SUPPORT

MEET THE TEAM

Create the structure for the company.

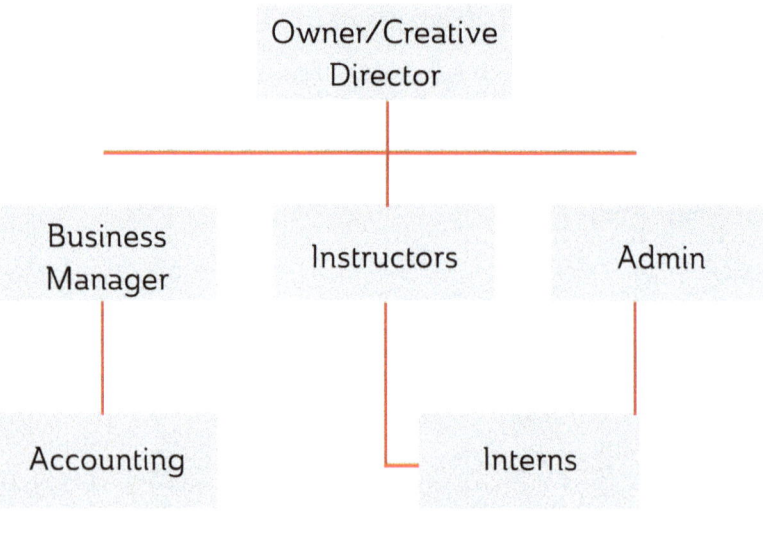

Notes

TEAM ROLES AND RESPONSIBILITIES

Write the roles and responsibilities of each employee.

Role / Responsibilities

Sarah Thompson: Overseeing creative direction, business development, and strategic planning.

Creative Instructors: Leading photography and painting workshops, classes, and events.

Administrative Staff: Managing studio operations, customer inquiries, scheduling, and marketing efforts.

TEAM ROLES AND RESPONSIBILITIES

Write the roles and responsibilities of each employee.

Add team member	Role	Responsibilities

Discover Your Calling

OUTREACH - MARKETING

Think of outreach and marketing in a business plan as the way you shout from the rooftops about your awesome business! It's super important because it's how you let people know you exist and convince them to buy what you're selling. Plus, it helps you build relationships with customers and grow your business.

To write about outreach and marketing, keep it simple and friendly:

1. Highlight Your Audience: Start by describing who your customers are and where you can find them. Are they young adults who love social media or busy parents who read magazines? Understanding your audience helps you tailor your marketing efforts to reach them.

2. Show Your Strategy: Explain how you plan to reach your customers and convince them to buy from you. Will you use social media, email marketing, or good old-fashioned flyers? Outline your tactics and why you think they'll work.

3. Focus on Benefits: Highlight the benefits of your products or services and why customers should choose you over the competition. Maybe you offer faster delivery, better quality, or a unique experience – whatever it is, make sure it shines!

4. Budget Wisely: Talk about how much money you're willing to spend on marketing and where it will go. Whether it's ads, promotions, or events, be realistic about what you can afford and what will give you the best bang for your buck.

5. *Measure Success:* Explain how you'll track the success of your marketing efforts. Will you look at sales numbers, website traffic, or social media engagement? Having metrics in place helps you see what's working and what needs tweaking.

By keeping it simple and friendly, you'll create a marketing plan that's easy to understand and exciting to implement. It's like laying the groundwork for spreading the word about your amazing business and watching it grow

OUTREACH - MARKETING

What is the need?

What are others doing?

Target Market
Who are you trying to help?

Key Statistics
Who is your demographic?

25-45
Target Age

F
Females

3+hrs
On Social Media Per Day

$80k
Average Yearly Income

45%
Shop Mobile Devices

8/10
Own A Business Or Personal Brand

Discover Your Calling

MARKETING PLAN

Method	Description	Budget
Write the marketing method here	Add a description of this method here	$123.00

Notes

REVENUE - RETENTION

Imagine revenue and customer retention in a business plan like the fuel and glue that keeps your business running smoothly! They're super important because they help you make money and keep your customers happy, which is key to long-term success.

To write about revenue and customer retention, keep it simple and friendly:

1. Focus on Making Money: Start by talking about how your business will generate income. Will it be through selling products, offering services, or maybe a combination of both? Explain your revenue streams and how you plan to make them grow over time.

2. Know Your Numbers: Be clear about your pricing strategy and how much money you expect to bring in. Crunch the numbers and show that you've done your homework. Investors and lenders love to see a solid financial plan!

3. Keep Customers Coming Back: Customer retention is all about keeping your customers happy and coming back for more. Talk about how you'll provide excellent customer service, build relationships, and encourage repeat business. Happy customers are loyal customers!

4. Show Your Appreciation: Explain how you'll show appreciation to your customers and keep them engaged. Maybe it's through loyalty programs, special offers, or personalized communication – whatever it is, make sure your customers know they're valued.

5. *Measure Success: Describe how you'll track your revenue and customer retention efforts. Will you look at sales numbers, customer feedback, or retention rates? Having metrics in place helps you see what's working and what needs improvement.*

By keeping it simple and friendly, you'll create a revenue and customer retention plan that's easy to understand and exciting to implement. It's like building a strong foundation for your business and setting yourself up for success in the long run!

SWOT ANALYSIS

SWOT analysis is like a superhero tool for businesses or even individuals! It helps you figure out your strengths, weaknesses, opportunities, and threats. Let's break it down:

S - Strengths: These are the things you're really good at. Maybe you're super organized or have awesome teamwork skills.

W - Weaknesses: These are areas where you could use a little improvement. It's totally okay! Maybe you struggle with time management or need to work on your public speaking.

O - Opportunities: These are like doors waiting to be opened! They're chances for you to grow and succeed. It could be a new job opening or a chance to learn a new skill.

T - Threats: These are things that could hold you back or cause trouble. It could be competition in your field or changes in the market.

So, SWOT analysis helps you look at all these things together to make smart decisions and plan your next moves like a pro!

Writing a SWOT list is straightforward and can be really helpful for gaining insights. Here's a simple guide:

Identify Your Purpose: Decide what you want to analyze. It could be a business, a project, or even yourself for personal development.

Create Four Sections: Draw a big square on a piece of paper

or create four columns on a digital document. Label each section with one of the letters: S for Strengths, W for Weaknesses, O for Opportunities, and T for Threats.

List Your Strengths: Think about what you or your subject does really well. These could be skills, resources, or advantages you have over others.

Identify Weaknesses: Be honest about areas that need improvement. What are you or your subject not so good at? What obstacles do you face?

Explore Opportunities: Consider external factors that could benefit you or your subject. Are there trends, changes, or openings in the market that you could take advantage of?

Recognize Threats: Look at potential risks or challenges in your environment. Are there competitors, economic factors, or other obstacles that could cause trouble?

Be Specific: Try to be as specific as possible when listing items in each section. This will help you later when you're analyzing your SWOT.

Keep It Balanced: Remember, a good SWOT analysis looks at both internal and external factors. Balance out your strengths and weaknesses with opportunities and threats to get a well-rounded view.

Review and Analyze: Once you've listed everything, take a step back and look at your SWOT as a whole. What patterns or insights do you notice? This will help you make informed decisions and plans for the future.

Take Action: Use your SWOT analysis to guide your next steps. Build on your strengths, address your weaknesses, seize opportunities, and mitigate threats. It's a powerful tool for strategic planning and decision-making!

Remember, SWOT analysis is flexible, so feel free to adjust it to fit your needs or situation. Have fun exploring and discovering new insights!

SWOT ANALYSIS IDEAS SPACE

Strengths
Enjoys challenges and dynamics of event planning Has start up money to self fund

Weaknesses
Fears change Uncertain of how to transition

Opportunities
Explore creative talents in photography and painting Turn her passion for event planning into a thriving business

Threats
Knows nothing about owning a multi-purpose space Knows nothing about business (permits, laws etc.),

SWOT ANALYSIS IDEAS SPACE

Strengths

_____

Weaknesses

_____

Opportunities

_____

Threats

_____

SARAH'S BASIC TWO-PAGE BUSINESS PLAN: WEEK ONE

Executive Summary:

Sarah Thompson is embarking on a journey to launch a creative studio in Los Angeles that specializes in photography and painting. Leveraging her passion for creativity and her background in corporate event planning, Sarah aims to create a space where individuals can explore their artistic talents, learn new skills, and connect with like-minded individuals. This business plan outlines Sarah's mission, business structure, target market, revenue model, and growth strategy for establishing and scaling her creative studio.

Mission Statement:

To inspire and empower individuals to unleash their creativity, express themselves through art, and build a vibrant community of artists in Los Angeles and beyond.

Organizational Structure:

Founder & Creative Director: Sarah Thompson

Creative Instructors

Administrative Staff

Roles and Responsibilities:

·Sarah Thompson: Overseeing creative direction, business development, and strategic planning.

·Creative Instructors: Leading photography and painting

workshops, classes, and events.

Administrative Staff: Managing studio operations, customer inquiries, scheduling, and marketing efforts.

Community Needs and Outreach:

Providing accessible and inclusive creative workshops and classes for individuals of all skill levels.

Hosting community events, exhibitions, and art shows to showcase local talent and foster artistic connections.

Partnering with schools, community centers, and non-profit organizations to offer art education programs and outreach initiatives.

Collaborating with local artists, businesses, and influencers to promote artistic expression and support the creative community.

Revenue and Customer Retention:

Workshop and Class Fees: Offering paid photography and painting workshops, classes, and private lessons.

Studio Memberships: Providing monthly or annual memberships for access to studio space, equipment, and exclusive events.

Art Sales: Selling original artworks, prints, and merchandise created by studio artists.

Event Rentals: Renting out studio space for private events, parties, and photo/video shoots.

Customer Retention Strategies: Implementing loyalty programs, referral discounts, and personalized communication to engage and retain customers.

GOALS:

One Month:

·Secure studio space and finalize lease agreements.

·Develop branding and marketing materials.

·Launch website and social media channels.

·Host a grand opening event to introduce the studio to the community.

Six Months:

·Build a diverse portfolio of photography and painting workshops and classes.

·Establish partnerships with local schools and organizations for outreach programs.

·Expand studio offerings to include additional art mediums and disciplines.

·Increase customer base and achieve positive feedback and reviews.

One Year:

·Achieve profitability and sustainable revenue growth.

·Cultivate a strong community of artists and students.

·Host regular art exhibitions and events.

·Enhance studio facilities and equipment based on customer feedback and demand.

Five Years:

·Expand to additional studio locations in neighboring cities.

- Offer online courses and virtual workshops for broader reach.

- Collaborate with renowned artists and industry experts for special events and programs.

- Establish the studio as a leading destination for artistic inspiration and education in the region.

MODULE 6
EVALUATION

CONCLUSION

There is no right or wrong way to use this book; there is merely an easier terrain to navigate if done in this order. I have tried to take shortcuts and reverse routes, but self-care is key to consistent forward movement into your calling when building, starting with a solid foundation. Your purpose is not linked to a profession, but your profession can showcase your purpose.

I hope you poured into, trusted, and provided purpose and plans for yourself. Thank you for trusting the process and doing it the way it was written. I know there were days when you stopped and wanted to quit, but you didn't. Sometimes, we need the break for the breakthrough as long as we don't turn it into a breakdown.

Continue to come back to steps you need to revisit or the whole book if your life takes a major overhaul.

M.I.S.S. METHOD (CREATED BY MAYA LYNNE ROBINSON)

MAKING --- SELF-CARE

Seven days of self-care to create a solid foundation for the mind, body, and spirit

INTERNAL - INTUITION

Seven days of intuition training using creativity, mindfulness, and trust techniques

SPIRITUAL - PURPOSE

Seven days of working to figure out what you are here to learn and teach

SHIFTS ----- PLAN

Seven days to solidify a 20-30 page business plan to live the life meant for you

WHAT I LEARNED

1. There is always more work to be done. I am not perfect. I am constantly evolving, and as I do, it shapes the people, places, and things around me.

2. Everything is a sign, especially when looking for one. Music quotes and numbers are my most instant confirmations.

3. You can get a lot done, personally, if you stay out of other people's business.

4. This is a journey of self, a journey of one. Even if you share it with others, every decision should be yours. Free will.

5. Go outside and turn your phone off for a little while. I deserve a little peace.

6. Because I constantly change, my goals and purpose may also change.

7. Even God rested. Take time away from outside influences if and when you can.

What did I learn about myself from this book?

_____

_____

_____

10 RULES I LIVE BY

1. I AM.

2. No matter someone's financial restraints, I will always find a way to work with them if they are ready and willing to work on themselves, too.

3. Energy is also a currency exchange.

4. Always tell the truth, so that I never have to remember a lie.

5. Happiness is freedom.

6. Trust my intuition- the first time.

7. Ask for and require honesty.

8. Leave people better than I found them.

9. The disrespect was the closure.

10. Speak, even when my voice shakes.

What rules do I live by?

_____

_____

_____

CERTIFICATE OF PURPOSE

This achievement is a reflection of consistency, discipline, and accountability. You can be proud of this accomplishment.

Presented to : _____

LIT IT'S YOUR LIFE

MAIN COURSE.

Reiki

Begin with a cup of tea, followed by a foot bath ritual while discussing your needs. Then, enjoy a soothing sound healing and a balancing Reiki session. In-person.

Reiki and a Reading

When you want balance and clarity.

Reiki and a Reading

Deep dive into limiting beliefs and traits that are holding you back.

CHEF'S SPECIALS.

Purpose Planner

This workbook will encourage you to remember the importance of "filling your cup first."

Discover Your Calling (Online Self-Paced Course)

Learn how to trust or retrust yourself again.

I Am On Purpose

Figuring out your blueprint and how to get you there. You are here for a reason.

Goal Planning

Learn how to give yourself long term vision and short term motivation.

RETREATS.

Soul Session Retreat

Reset Retreat

Virtual Retreat

RETAIL.

I Am (Affirmation Deck)

I Want (Shadow Work Deck)

Discover Your Calling

Glow

THANK-YOU!

There are many ways to improve your intuitive skills and live a more happy and peaceful life. Check out my site below for podcasts, blog posts, and other cool online support!

I'm so excited to continue working with you, please reach out to learn more.

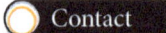

Contact

www.liveintruthspace.com
info@liveintruthspace.com

www.ingramcontent.com/pod-product-compliance
Lightning Source LLC
Chambersburg PA
CBHW061745070526
44585CB00025B/2807